BY THE SACKFUL

A Scrapbook with Recipes from
85 Years of White Castle Craving

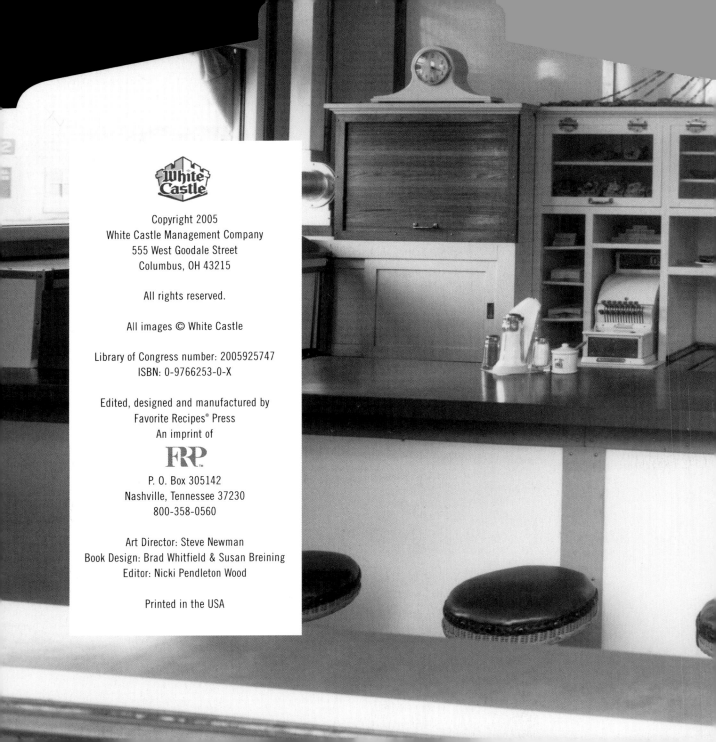

White Castle

Copyright 2005
White Castle Management Company
555 West Goodale Street
Columbus, OH 43215

Library of Congress number: 2005925747
ISBN: 0-9766253-0-X

Edited, designed and manufactured by
Favorite Recipes® Press
An imprint of

FRP

P. O. Box 305142
Nashville, Tennessee 37230
800-358-0560

Art Director: Steve Newman
Book Design: Brad Whitfield & Susan Breining
Editor: Nicki Pendleton Wood

Printed in the USA

Introduction

SALUTATIONS, CRAVER!

Thanks for opening our third compilation of recipes from fourteen years of contests and thousands of original and innovative recipe entries that reflect our fun customers and the quirky popularity of our little square burgers.

This is White Castle's first entry into the world of real books. It seemed like a special way to celebrate our eighty-fifth anniversary and our unique product and collect all our customers' creative recipes and fond memories of White Castle, plus lots of old photos, posters, and ads that we save for special occasions like this.

We found a fitting charity to support with sales of the book. As part of our ongoing commitment to help curb hunger and salute youth and entrepreneurship, we're donating profits for this book to Turkeys 4 America, which provides turkeys to needy families and is run by two enterprising teenagers.

White Castle is so lucky to have so many devoted followers. That's something other quick-serve restaurants can't claim, and we never forget it or take it for granted. (And naturally we hope the recipes inspire you to buy a sack of burgers and create your own recipe or enjoy one of ours!)

THE CRAVER RECIPE CONTESTS

FIRST RULE: Every recipe submitted to the contest uses ten White Castle hamburgers, including buns (but pickles optional). Finding a way to include the buns seems to bring out the true creativity in a cook, and it's always interesting to read the, um, innovative uses.

SOMETHING ELSE YOU SHOULD KNOW: Castle cooking inspires such clever titles, but some have been changed to keep things lively (most titles originally included the "White Castle" — not that we aren't flattered — but it is repetitive).

AND ONE OTHER ITEM: All the recipes here were award-winning concoctions and have at some point been prepared and tasted by one or another of the patient, hard-working panels of judges that we have engaged for the contests since 1991. (We're most grateful for one judge who has been with us since the first contest. Doral Chenoweth, the Grumpy Gourmet, is restaurant reviewer for *The Columbus Dispatch* and a faithful White Castle supporter.)

THE BEGINNING

You might be justified in wondering exactly how we got the idea for an annual recipe contest. Well, one Thanksgiving many years ago, a White Castle team member got quite inventive with her turkey stuffing, substituting crumbled burgers for the bread crumbs, and a new idea was born. Like the light of a star that travels for centuries to reach earth and illuminate the sky for all mankind, here's that long-ago recipe that continues to inspire further greatness:

The Original White Castle Turkey Stuffing

10 White Castle hamburgers, no pickles
1 1/2 cups diced celery
1 1/4 teaspoons thyme
1 1/2 teaspoons sage
3/4 teaspoon coarsely ground black pepper
1/4 cup chicken broth

Tear the burgers into large pieces and combine in a large bowl with the celery, thyme, sage and black pepper; toss to combine. Add the chicken broth and toss again. Stuff the mixture into the turkey cavity just before roasting. Makes about 9 cups, enough for a 10- to 12-pound turkey.

Note: Allow 1 hamburger for each pound of turkey, yielding about 3/4 cup stuffing per pound.

Hmm. Already there were urban legends circulating of a burger pâté, which just confirmed that there was something in the air. Something savory and delicious, perhaps lightly onion-flavored. The world was ready for whatever toothsome delights our culinary-minded customers could conjure.

We knew White Castle patrons were a fun-loving bunch, but we couldn't have guessed how far ranging their recipe ideas would be, or how long they would continue. Year after year, original recipes by the hundreds simply pour in. It's quite an extraordinary collection, as you'll see.

Then, when we were rooting around in a drawer for some party hats, we found some old pictures of early Castles and Cravers. It just seemed right to include them, and they tell a story that we hope is interesting. Or you could just scan the photos for familiar faces and cool vintage clothing.

Enjoy the book. Thanks for coming in. Keep it square.

Contents

It was a dark and stormy night. I've always wanted to start a love story with that aging literary bromide.
But when it comes to my professional career as a White Castle aficionado,
it started on a dark and stormy night. It started this way. The cop on the night beat needed coffee.
The reporter on the beat needed sustenance to make it to daylight.

In those days, half a century ago in my hometown, Columbus, Ohio, working the midnight shift of the afternoon
newspaper, cop house reporters had better relationships with the uniforms in police cruisers. We, as working stiffs,
rode the range of nighttime mean streets. My Downtown friend was Sgt. Bob Brush. We went on emergency runs
together. We talked about family, life, Ohio State football, politics, and crime. I went on runs with Brush
when he was trying to bring in a drunk driver. I went on runs with him when the police radio
ordered him to fires or accidents or crimes in progress.

My heart-stopping Brush memory was when the cop house radio sent him to a hostage situation. A guy with a gun in
his precinct was holding police at bay in the near Downtown. Sgt. Brush was second on the scene. The guy was
standing at the top of the stairs in a seedy flophouse. In those days we didn't have S. W. A. T. teams. We had cops in
uniforms, usually white shirts, black pants, guns and cuffs on thick leather belts. To shorten the story, Brush,
standing at the bottom of the staircase, began a calm conversation with the guy. He called him by name. He knew the
guy from previous runs. He knew his rap sheet by memory, but I did not. After some time with cruiser lights flashing,
Brush calmly said, "I'm coming up. Put down the gun. Everything will be fine. Just put down the gun...
don't drop it...neither of us want to be hurt, do we?"

That big cop slowly climbed the stairs, put his arm around the guy's shoulders, and helped him down to the street.
He told another cop to get the gun atop the stairs.

Brush turned to me and said, "Chenoweth, let's 56."

When an officer, even today, takes a shift break for a meal, he calls in to radio that he's "on a 56."
Brush and I did a 56 many nights. My first White Castle, then known as a slider—today trademarked
for protection of the cute usage as Slyder—came when Brush introduced me to the dark and stormy night
season of my new hometown. I've been hooked since...no regrets.

Time measured in decades and sacks of Castles seems to stand still when a Slyder is involved.
I continue addicted.

But today being a Slyder fancier has more meaning. I write about food, restaurants, people who make food for public consumption. Understand my food involvement. I've written about food and restaurants in several countries. I've been asked many times by publicity agencies to endorse a particular restaurant or food product. Of course, journalistic ethics prevent such. But, over the decades, I've always used my affinity for a high noon or a midnight Slyder as an escape route.

While being facetious and somewhat evasive, I get away from such requests by saying the only endorsement I make is for a Slyder. Since I'm writing as the Grumpy Gourmet for *The Columbus Dispatch,* one should assume my weekly columns on whatever subject are endorsements. White Castle System does not pay for my endorsements. They do nice things by annually inviting me to be a judge of the contests of recipes using a bag of Castles in the mix.

White Castle does nice things for me by never changing the recipe for the product in the box. That is nice for one so addicted to the aroma of steamed onions atop a bit of beef best described by size as a condiment for taste. White Castle moguls will never endorse my major use for a sack of six. I still call home at night, saying I am "on a 56." That soft, sweet, square bun with hot onions and just enough beef go so well with my favored burgundy. After all, I am in the privacy of my own home—ten blocks and ten minutes from my favorite 24/7/365 eatery.

White Castle, seriously, is my favorite food station for professional reasons. Twenty-four hours of availability is a saving grace in my eat-for-pay business. I am not a three-squares-a-day type. I eat/forage/hunt/gather/dine/sup when hunger pangs make sounds in the night.

So, a toast, coffee black, a 56 to an old cop buddy.

Doral Chenoweth is a food writer and lectures on the business of restaurants. His weekly column, RE$TAURANT$, appears in The Columbus Dispatch. *His teaching website on ethics of restaurant writing is* www.grumpygourmetusa.com.

The White Castle Pledge:

"Serving the finest products, for the least cost, in the cleanest surroundings,

with the most courteous personnel."

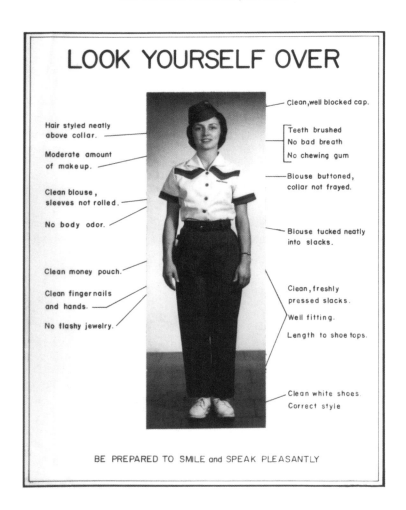

LOOK YOURSELF OVER

Clean, well blocked cap.

Hair styled neatly above collar.

Teeth brushed
No bad breath
No chewing gum

Moderate amount of makeup.

Blouse buttoned, collar not frayed.

Clean blouse, sleeves not rolled.

No body odor.

Blouse tucked neatly into slacks.

Clean money pouch.

Clean, freshly pressed slacks.

Well fitting.

Clean fingernails and hands.

Length to shoe tops.

No flashy jewelry.

Clean white shoes. Correct style

BE PREPARED TO SMILE and SPEAK PLEASANTLY

up and eat 'em

The Result of our Efforts to "Serve the Best Coffee in Town"

15,629,162 CUPS OF COFFEE

Sold in 1941 by **White Castle**

White Castle Christmas

*When I was honored as the 2000 Crave Time
Cook-Off Recipe Winner, I knew I was living the best year of my life.
Driving home from the award ceremony on a local TV show, I made a decision: I was going to
share my joy and have a White Castle Christmas. Instead of just dreaming of a white ...
CASTLE Christmas, I took several steps to make it happen.*

*1. Created one hundred Christmas ornaments out of the blue White Castle hamburger boxes. My husband spent
a month cutting and laminating my recipe to the bottom and back of the boxes. I then made Santa out of round
ornaments covered with felt, fur, curly hair, and bells. Besides hanging them all over our Christmas trees and
doorways, we gave away White Castle Santas, with Castle gift certificates, of course.*

*2. Put up outdoor decorations. We had two Christmas parties, one birthday party, and one retirement party
during the holidays. These required finding our house. This was easy for most, because it was the one with
a fifty-foot White Castle logo stretched across the entire house in blue twinkle lights and a sixteen-foot
"CRAVE" in lights across the fence.*

3. Used White Castle bags as gift wrap for smaller gifts and cut up Slyder boxes using all four sides as gift tags.

*4. Gave away my winning White Castle recipe to all who drove by the house! We painted an old
real estate sign to read "Free recipes" and taped burger boxes all over the sign.
More than two hundred Spicy White Castle Dip recipes were picked up over the holidays.*

*5. Turned a White Castle T-shirt into a holiday dress fit for a White Castle queen! I sewed shiny blue sequins
around the neck and safety-pinned a blue feather boa around the hem. A black turtleneck and tights
complemented the gown beautifully. "White Castle blue" high heels topped off my very special look.*

6. Fed Santa's crave! Gave him White Castle hamburgers and packed some for Rudolph!

*7. Had fun. White Castle is not just a restaurant, it's an experience!
This little burger in a box created a fun Christmas for my family!*

—Debbie Gardner, Loveland, Ohio

WHITE CASTLE COBBLER

White Castle Cobbler

10 White Castle cheeseburgers
4 eggs, beaten
1/2 cup milk
1/2 cup shredded Cheddar cheese
1/3 cup crisp-fried crumbled bacon
1 green bell pepper, chopped
1 teaspoon paprika
Salt and pepper to taste

Preheat the oven to 350 degrees. Remove and set
aside the top buns. Arrange the cheeseburgers in a
greased baking dish. Combine the eggs, milk and
cheese in a bowl. Soak the bun tops in this mixture
and replace them on top of the hamburgers. Pour the
remaining mixture over the hamburgers. Sprinkle the
cooked bacon, bell pepper, paprika, salt and pepper
on top. Bake until the mixture is set.
Makes 6 servings.

Steve T. Ridge, Danville, Illinois

Breakfast Castle Puff

10 White Castle cheeseburgers
3 eggs, beaten
2 cups milk
1/2 cup chopped onion
1/2 cup chopped green bell pepper
1 teaspoon dry mustard
3/4 teaspoon garlic salt
1/4 teaspoon black pepper
Grated taco cheese
Paprika

Preheat the oven to 350 degrees. Cut the
cheeseburgers into halves and place them in a
9x13-inch baking dish. Combine the eggs, milk,
onion, bell pepper, dry mustard, garlic salt and
pepper in a bowl and mix well.

Pour over the cheeseburgers. Sprinkle with taco
cheese and paprika. Cover with plastic wrap
and refrigerate overnight or for approximately
1 hour. Remove the plastic wrap and bake for 45 to
50 minutes or until set. Makes 6 to 8 servings.

N. R. Wisser, Prior Lake, Minnesota

Santa's Favorite

One snowy Christmas Eve about 10 o'clock, we were on our way home for the evening. "Oh no! We don't have any cookies for Santa," I said to my husband. Our 3-year-old son started to cry. "He won't come now," he said. We looked around for a party store. Nothing was open. Then we saw a White Castle. It was open! We stopped and bought two burgers. "Santa will like our house best," our son said. We set the burgers on the cookie plate with a beer.

We've done that every year since. Our son is 5 1/2 now and if you ask him what Santa likes best, he'll say, "Two White Castle burgers and a beer!"

—William, Christina, & Joshua Thomason, Dearborn, Michigan

Hamburger Quiche

10 White Castle hamburgers
6 slices bacon, cooked crisp and crumbled
1 cup (4 ounces) shredded Cheddar cheese
4 large eggs
1 cup half-and-half

Preheat the oven to 350 degrees. Cut each hamburger into 4 pieces and press firmly into a lightly buttered 9-inch pie plate. Sprinkle the bacon and cheese over the hamburger pieces. Beat the eggs and half-and-half in a large bowl; pour over the bacon and cheese. Bake until set, 35 to 40 minutes. Let stand 10 minutes before serving. Makes 6 servings.

Marge Walker, Santa Claus, Indiana

This little 1921 block building (with just five stools) in Wichita, Kansas, is considered the first White Castle, meaning it was the first restaurant operated under the partnership of Walt Anderson and Billy Ingram. *Probably a leased property, the restaurant closed in October 1927.*

Microwave Castle Onion Ring Quiche

10 White Castle bacon cheeseburgers
1¹/₃ cups milk
10 eggs, lightly beaten
Salt and pepper to taste
Tabasco sauce (optional)

Chopped green onions (optional)
Italian spices (optional)
Shredded cheese (optional)
White Castle onion rings
Tomato wedges

Lightly grease 2 microwave-safe 9-inch pie plates. Remove the pickles from the bacon cheeseburgers. (Regular hamburgers or cheeseburgers may be substituted.) Arrange 4 whole bacon cheeseburgers in each pie plate. Cut the remaining 2 bacon cheeseburgers diagonally both ways for a total of 8 pieces. Use these to fill the spaces between the whole hamburgers.

Microwave the milk in a bowl on HIGH for 1 to 1¹/₂ minutes or until small bubbles form around the edge. Add the eggs and beat well. Add salt, pepper, Tabasco sauce, green onions, Italian spices and shredded cheese. Pour half the mixture into each pie plate. Microwave each quiche on MEDIUM for 7 to 8 minutes, then let stand for 3 minutes. Remove to a serving plate. Garnish with White Castle onion rings and tomato wedges. Recipe may be halved. Makes 8 to 10 servings.

Peg & John Baird, Norwalk, Ohio

Stubby's 3-Cheese Spinach Quiche

10 White Castle hamburgers
1 pound bacon, cooked and crumbled
1 small onion, chopped
1 medium green bell pepper, chopped
8 to 12 ounces ham, cut into pieces
12 eggs
1 tablespoon milk or water
Salt, black pepper, red hot pepper sauce and
chopped parsley to taste

1 pound frozen chopped spinach,
   thawed and cooked
10 slices Cheddar cheese, cut into pieces
10 slices American cheese,
   cut into pieces
10 slices Swiss cheese, cut into pieces
3 (9-inch) prepared pie shells

Preheat the oven to 350 degrees. Remove the buns from the hamburgers and chop the meat. Combine the meat, bacon, onion, bell pepper and ham in a large bowl and mix well.

Beat the eggs, milk, salt, pepper, hot sauce and parsley in a large bowl with an electric mixer until frothy. Add the spinach and cheeses and mix well. Spoon the meat mixture into the pie shells and top with the egg mixture. Bake for 45 minutes or until set. Cool and serve.

Joseph F. Cittadino, Valley Stream, New York

White Castle's medieval motif was inspired by Chicago's famous Water Tower.

Burger and Cheese Quiche

1 tablespoon vegetable oil
1 medium onion, chopped
1/2 teaspoon each tarragon, thyme and parsley
Salt and pepper to taste
1 pound shredded mild Swiss cheese
(about 4 cups)

6 eggs
2 1/2 cups whole milk
1/2 teaspoon nutmeg
2 prepared refrigerated pie pastries
10 White Castle hamburgers

Preheat the oven to 425 degrees. Heat the oil in a small skillet and sauté the onion, tarragon, thyme and parsley until the onion begins to color. Season with salt and pepper. Remove from heat and cool.

Combine the onion mixture with the shredded cheese and set aside. Beat the eggs, milk, nutmeg, salt and pepper in a large bowl. Combine 1 of the pie pastries with 3/4 of the other to form a large ball. Discard the remaining dough. Roll the ball into a 16-inch circle on a generously floured surface. Fit the pastry into a greased or nonstick 10-inch springform pan and trim edges as needed.

Spread 1 cup of the cheese over the pie crust. Top with the hamburgers around the edge, then sprinkle with the remaining cheese, filling in the gaps between the hamburgers and in the center; reserve a handful of the cheese for the top of the quiche. Pour the egg mixture evenly over the hamburgers. Sprinkle the remaining cheese over the hamburgers that protrude above the egg mixture.

Bake for 15 minutes, then reduce the heat to 375 degrees and bake for 45 minutes longer or until the center is set and the protruding burgers are brown and crispy. Let stand for 15 minutes. Remove to a serving plate. Makes 10 servings.

Aldo Fusaro, Clarendon Hills, Illinois

Chicago # 7 opened September 1922. Notice the old building on the left (a glazed brick construction) and the edge of the new building on the right (a "water tower" castle, designed after the Chicago Water Tower). As White Castles were updated, its location remained open while the new building was built on the same property, offering dining and a show.

Chili Cheese Olé

10 White Castle hamburgers, cut into halves
4 (4-ounce) cans chopped green chiles
8 ounces each shredded Cheddar cheese and
Monterey Jack cheese, divided
2 green onions, thinly sliced
6 to 8 black olives, chopped
1 (10-ounce) can diced tomatoes with green chiles
1 cup flour
5 eggs
3 1/2 cups half-and-half
Salt and pepper to taste

Grease a deep glass baking dish large enough to hold the hamburgers. Spread half the green chiles in the dish. Layer with the hamburger halves, half of the cheese, and the remaining chiles and cheese. Sprinkle the green onions and black olives over the top. Pour the tomatoes with green chiles over the layers.

Combine the flour, eggs, half-and-half, salt and pepper in a bowl. Pour the mixture over the whole dish. Bake for 1 hour. Cut into squares and serve with sour cream and salsa.

Zita Wilensky, North Miami, Florida

Scrumptious King's Delight

10 White Castle hamburgers
1 tablespoon shortening
8 to 10 medium potatoes, chopped
1 medium onion, diced
2 tablespoons salt
2 tablespoons black pepper
4 eggs, lightly beaten
1 (8-ounce) package sharp American
cheese, shredded
1 (1-pound) box Velveeta, shredded
1 pound bacon, cooked and crumbled

Preheat the oven to 350 degrees. Arrange the hamburgers (including buns) side by side in a greased casserole dish large enough for them to fit in 1 layer. Melt the shortening in a skillet and fry the potatoes with the onion, salt and pepper, but do not allow them to brown. Drain and spread the potatoes over the hamburgers. Top with the eggs, American cheese, Velveeta and bacon. Cover with foil and bake for 30 minutes or until set. Remove the foil and bake for 15 minutes longer or until lightly browned.

Tamula M. Tucker, Louisville, Kentucky

In the 1920s, local bakeries and butchers made daily, or even twice daily, deliveries of meat and bread. The food was fresh, *but cofounder Billy Ingram wanted buns to taste the same at every location, so the company eventually opened its own bakeries.*

Company Eggs Foo Young

1/4 cup cornstarch
1/2 cup cold water
4 cups beef broth
1/3 cup soy sauce
10 White Castle hamburgers, no pickles
1/4 cup vegetable oil, divided
1 tablespoon Szechuan sauce

1 cup diced green bell pepper
1/2 cup diced celery
1 large onion, diced
3 cups fresh or canned bean sprouts
8 to 10 large eggs
Hot cooked rice

Dissolve the cornstarch in cold water, stirring to form a paste. Heat the beef broth in a saucepan and add the soy sauce. When the broth mixture is hot but not boiling, add the cornstarch paste. Cook until the mixture thickens, stirring constantly. Simmer over very low heat or cover and keep warm.

Remove the hamburgers from the buns and chop the the meat; cut the buns into cubes. Heat 2 tablespoons of the oil in a wok or large skillet and add the Szechuan sauce. Cook for 10 seconds, then add the hamburger meat. Cook for 1 to 2 minutes or until the meat is hot and well-coated with sauce, stirring constantly. Remove the mixture from the pan and set aside. Heat the remaining oil and stir-fry the bell pepper, celery, and onion for 3 to 5 minutes or until tender-crisp. Add the bean sprouts and stir-fry for 2 minutes longer. Set aside. Beat the eggs in a large bowl. Add the cooked meat, cubed buns and cooked vegetables and mix well.

Grease a non-stick skillet or griddle and heat over medium heat. Spoon the egg mixture into "pancakes," cooking 3 to 4 at a time. Cook until brown, then turn and brown the other side. Remove from the skillet and keep warm. Serve over rice, topped with sauce.

Dean Baldwin, Erie, Pennsylvania

Breakfast Enchiladas

2 tablespoons vegetable oil	2 1/2 cups shredded Cheddar cheese, divided
1 red bell pepper, finely chopped	1 carton egg substitute (equal to 4 eggs)
1 bunch (about 8) green onions, sliced thin	2 cups half-and-half
10 White Castle hamburgers, no pickles, chopped	1 tablespoon all-purpose flour
	3 drops hot pepper sauce
8 (8-inch) flour tortillas	Sour cream and salsa

Preheat the oven to 350 degrees. Heat the oil in a large skillet and sauté the bell pepper and green onions until tender. Remove from the heat and add the hamburgers, mixing well. Place 1/3 cup of the mixture down the center of each of the tortillas. Top with 3 tablespoons cheese and roll to enclose.
Place seam-side down in a greased 9x13-inch baking dish.

Beat the remaining ingredients in a large bowl and pour over the enchiladas. Cover and refrigerate overnight. Bake, uncovered, for 30 minutes or until a knife inserted in the center comes out clean. Sprinkle with the remaining cheese. Serve with sour cream and salsa. Makes 8 enchiladas.

Adam Takessian, Washington, District of Columbia

White Castle began packaging its small, square burgers in paperboard cartons in 1931 to keep them warm and to keep them from being crushed inside the paper sacks. Each carton included reheating instructions to educate the public on this exotic, newfangled foodstuff.

Bacon Tot Bake

10 White Castle hamburgers
2 pounds frozen tater tots
1 pound bacon, cooked and crumbled
1 (10-ounce) can cream of mushroom soup
1 soup can milk
1 1/2 cups shredded Cheddar cheese

Preheat the oven using the directions on the package of tater tots. Layer the hamburgers, buns and all, in the bottom of a rectangular baking dish. Combine the tater tots, bacon, soup and milk in a large bowl and mix well. Layer over the hamburgers. Bake the mixture using the tater tot package directions. Remove from the oven 5 minutes before the recommended baking time and top with the cheese. Bake for 5 minutes longer or until the cheese is melted.

Dana Brown, Kansas City, Missouri

According to some experts, the french fry was not invented by the French, but the Belgians.

BELGIAN FRIES?

Queen's Breakfast Casserole

8 ounces fresh mushrooms, cut into halves
1 large onion, chopped
3 tablespoons butter
8 eggs
2 cups milk
Salt and pepper to taste
8 to 12 ounces shredded Monterey Jack and
Cheddar cheese blend
10 White Castle hamburgers

Preheat the oven to 350 degrees. Grease a 9x13-inch baking dish. Sauté the mushrooms and onion in the butter in a large skillet until tender. Beat the eggs, milk, salt and pepper in a large bowl until well blended. Add the cheese and mix well. Arrange the hamburgers in the baking dish. Cover with the mushroom mixture. Pour the egg mixture over all. Bake for 30 minutes or until set. Serve with golden potatoes or home fries and a fresh fruit salad.

Nicole DiSalvo, Nashville, Tennessee

Hash Bash

1/2 bag (about 1 pound) frozen shredded
hash brown potatoes
10 White Castle hamburgers, no pickles
1 green bell pepper, thinly sliced
1 onion, thinly sliced
1 (8-ounce) bag shredded Cheddar cheese

Preheat the oven to 350 degrees. Spread the hash brown potatoes in a greased 9x13-inch baking pan. Arrange the bottoms of the buns and the meat patties evenly on top of the potatoes. Layer with the bell pepper and onion. Sprinkle the cheese evenly over the mixture. Top with the bun tops (2 rows of 5). Cover loosely with foil.

Bake for 35 minutes or until the pepper and onion are tender and the hash brown potatoes are cooked. Cut into 10 portions and serve 2 portions to each person. Makes 5 servings.

Edna Manganello, Wood Dale, Illinois

The average American eats nearly 10,000 lbs. of potatoes in their lifetime.

Vegetable Hash

1 medium carrot, shredded
1 small onion, diced
$1/2$ garlic clove, pressed
1 green bell pepper, diced
1 red bell pepper, diced
4 tablespoons vegetable oil
7 medium potatoes, diced
10 White Castle hamburgers
$1/4$ cup shredded Cheddar cheese
$1/4$ cup water
2 tomatoes, diced

Preheat the oven to 300 degrees. Sauté the carrot, onion, garlic and bell peppers in hot oil in a skillet over medium heat. Add the potatoes and sauté until tender, stirring frequently. Line the bottom of a 9x13-inch baking pan with the hamburgers, setting aside the bun tops and pickles. Spread the sautéed vegetables over the hamburgers. Crumble the bun tops over the vegetables and sprinkle the cheese over the mixture. Pour the water over everything. Bake for 30 to 45 minutes. Garnish with the pickles and diced tomatoes.

Teri Smith, Kansas City, Missouri

Spud Brunch Bake

10 White Castle hamburgers, torn into small pieces
5 cups diced potatoes
2 cups (8 ounces) shredded Cheddar cheese, divided
4 eggs, beaten
2 tablespoons melted margarine
Salt and pepper to taste
Hot red pepper sauce (optional)

Preheat the oven to 350 degrees. Combine the hamburger pieces, potatoes, $1 1/2$ cups of the cheese, the eggs, margarine, salt and pepper in a large bowl and mix well. Pour into a casserole and top with the remaining cheese. Bake for 1 hour or until the center is set.

Tina Dennis, Stoutsville, Ohio

Castle Breakfast Quiche

10 White Castle hamburgers
3/4 cup shredded sharp Cheddar cheese
3 tablespoons chopped onion
1 medium zucchini, grated
6 eggs
2 cups lowfat milk
1 teaspoon salt
1/4 cup margarine, melted

Preheat the oven to 400 degrees. Line a greased
9x13-inch baking pan with the hamburgers, removing the
top buns. Layer the cheese, onion, and zucchini over the
hamburgers. Replace the top buns.

Beat the eggs with the milk, salt and margarine in
a large bowl. Pour over the hamburgers. Cover and chill
in the refrigerator for at least 8 hours.

Bake for 45 minutes or until set.

Juanita Helton, Bloomington, Illinois

have a little friend for lunch

Some children were raised with a silver spoon in their mouths.
I had the fortune of growing up with a White Castle hamburger in mine.

Just a few blocks from my home was the Castle of my dreams sitting on a corner. The little delicacies cost five cents each. It was a taste bud delight, and we dined there about twice a month. This Castle seated six people, and many times we ate standing at the window enjoying the unique taste and watching the traffic.

On the next block was our favorite movie theater. My friend and I went there each Saturday afternoon. One day, we decided to sneak some burgers into the theater. "Sneak" is the word because no food other than the concessions was welcomed by the manager. We brought a brown bag from home to disguise our lunch. The big shot took our tickets that day and said, "What's in the bag, girls?" We were only about ten years old and this frightened us half to death. I immediately lied and said, "We bought some S. O. S. pads to clean the pots and pans when we get home." (The S. O. S. pads were about the size of our bag.) Quick thinking on my part! He allowed the lie to stand and motioned us in.

WE DID IT! WE SMUGGLED WHITE CASTLES INTO THE THEATER!

We were so afraid he would check on us that we tore off a bite of the burger and dipped our hands into the popcorn box as though that was all we were eating. That was so we wouldn't be suspected of any theater felony. That was the way we ate our lunch that day, with our hearts beating far too fast for comfort. If we'd been caught, we might have lost the opportunity to ever come back to see Tarzan and Jane. We were taking a big chance. Were the White Castles worth the risk? Of course they were. I'd do it again in a heartbeat.

I am now sixty years old and dine at my favorite Castle once a week. Put a little mustard on my burger and complement it with a Coke and I am in hamburger heaven. Would I trade my White Castles for that silver spoon? No way. I am happy feeling like a princess in the White Castle.

—Marilyn Kloncz, Eagan, Minnesota

Spicy Cheese Dip

1 (8-ounce) package cream cheese
3 White Castle Dusseldorf mustard packets
1/2 cup finely chopped onion
10 White Castle hamburgers
9 ounces pepper Jack cheese, cut into chunks
2/3 cup milk
2 tablespoons parsley flakes
Tortilla chips

Combine the cream cheese and mustard and spread in the bottom of a large, shallow microwaveable serving dish. Spread the onions evenly on top. Process the hamburgers in a food processor until finely chopped and then spread over the onions.

Combine the cheese and milk in a microwave-safe bowl or cup and microwave for 1 to 2 minutes or until the cheese is melted. Stir until smooth, then pour over the hamburger layer. Sprinkle with the parsley flakes. Microwave on HIGH for 3 to 4 minutes, or bake in a 350-degree oven for 30 minutes. Serve with tortilla chips.

Debbie Gardner, Loveland, Ohio

Salsa Dip

1 (8-ounce) package cream cheese, softened
10 White Castle hamburgers
1 (16-ounce) jar salsa
1 (8-ounce) package shredded Cheddar cheese
Tortilla chips

Preheat the oven to 350 degrees. Spread the cream cheese over the bottom of an 8-inch pie plate. Crumble the hamburgers and mix with the salsa. Pour the mixture over the cream cheese. Sprinkle with the cheese and bake for 30 minutes or until heated through. Serve with tortilla chips.

Robert Whitely, Stamford, Connecticut

Restaurant managers were called "operators" and usually worked alone. Here, an operator protects his Castle, probably late 1920s.

Early White Castle locations were built in this water tower style from porcelain steel, but soon the building materials would change, then change again.

Vidalia Onion Dip

14 White Castle hamburgers, buns removed and reserved, meat chopped fine
2^1/$_2$ cups chopped Vidalia onions
1^3/$_4$ cup mayonnaise
2 cups shredded Swiss cheese
^{1}/$_2$ cup cooked, crumbled bacon
Crackers

Preheat the oven to 350 degrees. Combine the hamburger pieces, onions, mayonnaise, cheese and bacon and mix well. Spoon the mixture into a baking dish. Bake for 30 to 35 minutes; let stand 10 minutes. Toast the buns. Serve the dip hot with the toasted buns and crackers.

Karen Walkup, Norcross, Georgia

White Castle Pâté

10 White Castle hamburgers
^{1}/$_4$ cup steak sauce
2 tablespoons Worcestershire sauce
1 tablespoon sweet mustard
2 tablespoons sweet barbecue sauce
1 teaspoon hot red pepper sauce
Crackers

Combine all the ingredients in a blender (pickles, buns, everything) and process until very finely chopped and thoroughly blended. Form the mixture into a ball. Chill thoroughly in the refrigerator. Serve with crackers.

Earl Spicer, St. Louis, Missouri

5-Layer Bean Dip

10 White Castle hamburgers, no pickles
2 envelopes taco seasoning mix
1 (15-ounce) can refried beans
1 (4-ounce) can diced jalapeño peppers
2 cups shredded Cheddar cheese
1 cup sour cream
Tortilla chips

Chop the hamburgers; combine with one envelope of the taco seasoning and set aside. Spread the refried beans evenly over a large plate. Top with the meat mixture, jalapeño peppers and cheese. Microwave until the cheese melts. Combine the remaining envelope of taco seasoning with the sour cream and use the mixture to top the dip. Serve with tortilla chips.

Travis Cloutier, Minneapolis, Minnesota

Cheesy Crave Dip

2 pounds Velveeta
1/4 cup milk
1 1/4-ounce package chili seasoning mix
2 tablespoons hot red pepper sauce
8 ounces medium salsa
1/4 cup sliced jalapeño peppers
10 White Castle hamburgers
Tortilla chips

Melt the cheese in a 5-quart slow-cooker, adding the milk to prevent scorching. Add the chili seasoning packet, hot sauce, salsa and jalapeño slices. Remove the top buns of the hamburgers and cut the meat into small pieces. Add to the cheese mixture and mix well. Serve with tortilla chips.

John Wilper, Hillsboro, Missouri

30

Royal Romance

In 1966, I met a man named Lloyd. He worked the late shift, so when we went out, the only place that was always open was White Castle. We loved White Castles almost as much as we loved each other. We dated like this for quite a while, but we broke up. I also worked at the time and made $1.65 an hour. On almost all my paydays, I would take my mom and six younger brothers and sisters out to eat, always to White Castle. It made me miss Lloyd so much.

One payday, about nine months after Lloyd and I had broken up, I was standing in line at White Castle when my little twin brothers told me that I should look behind us. When I turned around and saw Lloyd smiling at me, I knew I still loved him. I gave my family their food and I went and sat with him. We ate White Castles and talked about our future.

This year we will celebrate our thirty-second wedding anniversary. Lloyd's family told me after we were married that he had said he just had to go back to his White Castle-eating girl. And after all these years, two daughters, and a granddaughter, we still love each other, and we still love White Castle.

—Debbie Martin, Indianapolis, Indiana

Vicki's Bacon Cheese Puff Appetizer

20 strips bacon
10 White Castle hamburgers, no pickles
4 ounces whipped cream cheese with chives
(or any cream cheese flavor)

Preheat the oven to 350 degrees. Cut the bacon strips into halves to make 40 strips. Partially cook the bacon, then drain on paper towels. Remove the bun top and spread 2 teaspoons of the cream cheese on each meat patty. Replace the buns. Cut each hamburger into quarters. Wrap a bacon strip around each quarter with the open ends of bacon on the bottom. Bake on a nonstick baking sheet for 8 minutes. Makes 40 pieces.

Vicki Gazdick, New York, New York

Special Delivery

It was 1 a.m. and I was 8½ months pregnant with my second child. My husband Ray used to sense that I was awake and was especially worried about my going into labor. He also suffered sympathy pains with me, calling from work to ask me about a sudden pain so we could compare.

I had an unbearable craving for White Castle hamburgers. He was awake, and I told him. Next thing I know, he's pulling on his clothes to go out for burgers. I protested, but he kissed me and insisted that if I had a craving, he would take care of it. He drove off to get the burgers.

We had an old car with a broken gas gauge and Ray ran out of gas. He got out and began walking, not in the direction of home, but toward the White Castle. A policeman stopped to ask what was wrong and Ray explained the situation. But he didn't finish the story, because the officer understood the situation immediately, took him to the White Castle, then to the gas station, then back to the car.

Because of the romance, those were the best White Castles I ever had. Ray always joked that he treated me like a queen because he took me to White Castle—I have no argument with that. After 37 years of marriage and a lot of romantic moments, that's still my favorite.

Another 1920s operator showing off his Castle. The restaurants were often built on leased property, and would move or close upon the termination of the lease. This allowed the company to follow the population as workplaces moved.

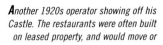

Won Tons

10 White Castle hamburgers
1 package won ton wrappers
$1/4$ cup soy sauce plus $1/2$ cup for serving
$1/8$ teaspoon minced fresh ginger
6 sliced green onions
2 garlic cloves, minced
Peanut oil for frying or water for steaming

Cut the hamburgers into fourths. Place a hamburger quarter on a won ton wrapper. Sprinkle with the next 4 ingredients. Draw the won ton into a bundle. Wet fingers and press edges to seal. Repeat the procedure until the remaining ingredients are used.

For crispy fried won tons, heat at least 1 inch of oil in a deep pot and fry the won tons, a few at a time, until lightly browned. For soft steamed won tons, bring water to a boil in a large pot. Place the won tons into a steamer basket, cover with a lid, and lower the basket into a position over, not in, the water. Steam the won tons until they are the consistency of cooked pasta. Serve with soy sauce.

Martha Buhl, Purdys, New York

Dim Sum

10 White Castle hamburgers, no ketchup
$1/2$ cup sliced green onions
2 tablespoons finely chopped garlic
2 tablespoons shredded gingerroot
1 tablespoon soy sauce
Soy sauce, duck sauce and hot mustard for dipping

Separate the buns from the hamburgers. Scrape the cooked onions from the buns and reserve both. With a rolling pin, flatten the buns to $1/8$-inch thickness. Chop the meat and cooked onions into small pieces. Combine in a large bowl with the green onions, garlic and gingerroot. Add the soy sauce and mix well. Divide the meat mixture into 20 equal parts and place in the center of each flattened bun. Pull the 4 corners of the flattened bun up around the meat and pinch closed. Place in a bamboo steamer for 5 minutes. Serve hot with soy sauce, duck sauce and hot mustard for dipping.

David Bashford, Westfield, New Jersey

Castle-Stuffed Portobellos

1 pound medium portobello mushrooms
1/4 cup olive oil
1/2 teaspoon garlic powder
1/2 teaspoon black pepper
10 White Castle hamburgers
1/2 cup shredded Parmesan cheese

Wipe the mushrooms clean. Remove the stems and chop coarsely. Mix the oil, garlic powder and black pepper and brush the mixture on the mushroom caps. Reserve any leftover oil.

Heat a skillet over medium-high heat and add the mushrooms, bottom side down. Brown slightly. Remove from the skillet and set aside. Heat the remaining oil and cook the chopped stems until the moisture is cooked out. Chop the hamburgers coarsely and combine with the stems and Parmesan cheese. Stuff the caps with the mixture and broil the caps until the cheese is melted.

Debbie Lyons, Valparaiso, Indiana

Stuffed Mushrooms Parmigiana

2 pounds fresh mushrooms
10 White Castle hamburgers, crumbled
20 slices pepperoni, finely chopped
1/4 cup finely diced bell pepper, any color
2 garlic cloves, minced
3 tablespoons chopped fresh parsley
1/4 teaspoon seasoned salt
1/4 teaspoon dried oregano, crushed
Dash black pepper
2/3 cup chicken broth

Preheat the oven to 325 degrees. Remove the stems from the mushrooms and discard. Place the mushroom caps on a large baking sheet with a lip, such as a jellyroll pan. Combine the hamburgers, pepperoni, bell pepper, garlic, parsley, salt, oregano and black pepper and mix well. Add the chicken broth and mix well. Stuff the mixture into the mushroom caps. Pour about 1/8 inch water into the pan. Bake for 20 minutes or until the mushrooms are tender. Makes about 60 stuffed mushrooms.

Kathie DiPaolo, Columbus, Ohio

Sweet and Spicy Meatballs

10 White Castle hamburgers, no pickles
2 eggs
1 tablespoon pepper
2 to 3 tablespoons Worcestershire sauce
2 (18-ounce) jars grape jelly
2 (16-ounce) bottles chili sauce

Preheat the oven to 350 degrees.
Remove the buns and set aside. Grind the hamburgers
and buns separately. Combine the hamburger meat,
eggs, pepper and Worcestershire sauce in a bowl with
enough of the ground buns until the mixture is
stiff. Roll the mixture into small balls. Place the meatballs
on a baking sheet and bake for 15 minutes, turning
halfway through baking.

Combine the grape jelly and chili sauce in a slow
cooker and add the meatballs. Heat and eat.

Kathy Christiansen, St. Peters, Missouri

Kingly Meatballs

10 White Castle hamburgers
1/4 cup chopped onion
2 egg whites
1 teaspoon ground sage
1 garlic clove, minced
1/2 teaspoon salt
Dash of black pepper

1 cup jellied cranberry sauce
1/2 cup orange marmalade
1/2 cup pineapple juice
1/4 cup ketchup
2 tablespoons packed brown sugar
1 tablespoon Worcestershire sauce

Preheat the oven to 400 degrees. Remove the meat patties from the buns. Crumble the meat. Toast and crumble the buns. Combine the meat patties with the onion, egg whites, sage, garlic, salt and pepper and mix well. Form small portions of the mixture into meatballs. Place in a single layer in a deep baking dish. Bake for 10 minutes. Meanwhile, combine the cranberry sauce, orange marmalade, pineapple juice, ketchup, brown sugar and Worcestershire sauce in a medium bowl and mix well. Pour over the meatballs. Bake for 20 minutes longer.

Debra Hart, Columbus, Ohio

Which is bigger, the boss's car, or the boss's restaurant? Walter Anderson, left, and Billy Ingram, right, in front of Wichita, Kansas, Castle No. 10 (opened May 1925, closed July 1929) with their totally cool Franklin automobiles. In 1957, Ingram would be acknowledged as "Grandaddy of the Hamburger" for his fast food vision.

Kastle Kabobs

10 White Castle hamburgers
10 cherry tomatoes
10 fresh mushrooms
2 orders White Castle onion chips or rings
5 packets White Castle Dusseldorf mustard
1 tablespoon soft margarine

Preheat a gas or charcoal grill or broiler. Remove the pickles from the hamburgers and reserve. Cut the hamburgers into quarters. Thread 8 quarters, 2 tomatoes, 2 mushrooms, some of the pickles and onion chips or rings onto each skewer, alternating them. Mix the mustard and margarine in a bowl.

Prepare a double layer of aluminum foil large enough to enclose each kabob. Spread some of the mustard mixture down the center of each foil sheet. Place a kabob over the mustard mixture and wrap securely. Heat the kabobs on the grill for 15 to 20 minutes or until hot, turning occasionally.

Elizabeth M. Urick, Logansport, Indiana

Royal Crave Slyder Bread

2 (1-pound) tubes refrigerated pizza dough
10 White Castle hamburgers, no pickles, no ketchup
3 large eggs
1 pound grated mozzarella cheese
3/4 cup grated Parmesan cheese
2 teaspoons each dried basil and oregano
1/2 teaspoon dried rosemary
1/2 teaspoon sage
1/2 teaspoon salt
1/4 teaspoon ground cloves
1/4 teaspoon allspice
1/4 teaspoon black pepper

Preheat the oven to 375 degrees. Roll the pizza dough into 1/4-inch thick rectangles on a lightly floured surface. Break up the hamburgers into very small pieces and mix the meat with the eggs, cheeses, herbs, salt and black pepper. Spoon the meat mixture onto each dough rectangle. Roll to enclose the filling, pinch the seams to seal them. Place the rolls on a lightly greased baking sheet, seam side down, and bake for 40 minutes or until crusty and brown. Cool on a wire rack and cut into slices.

Kenny Schrader, Edison, New Jersey

Cofounder Billy Ingram said he hoped "to hire young men between the ages of eighteen and twenty-four years old, of neat appearance, good character, *and preferably with a high school education." That worked fine until World War II, when those nice young men were otherwise occupied.*

Castle Cornbread

1¹/4 cups flour
³/4 cup cornmeal
¹/2 teaspoon tarragon
1 egg, beaten
1¹/4 cups milk
3 tablespoons butter
1 (12-ounce) can whole kernel corn, drained
2 or 3 White Castle hamburgers,
meat and onions only

Preheat the oven to 400 degrees. Grease an 8-inch square baking pan. Combine the flour, cornmeal and tarragon in a bowl and mix well. Stir in the egg, milk, butter and corn. Add the hamburgers and onions and mix lightly. Spoon the batter into the pan. Bake for 20 to 25 minutes or until a tester inserted in the center comes out clean.

Doral Chenoweth, The Grumpy Gourmet, Columbus Dispatch, Columbus, Ohio

Hamburger Hush Puppies

10 White Castle hamburgers
1 cup yellow cornmeal
1 teaspoon salt
1 teaspoon black pepper
3 eggs, slightly beaten
Hot red pepper sauce (optional)
Paprika to taste (optional)
Peanut oil

Remove the pickles from the hamburgers and chop finely. Tear the hamburgers into small pieces. Combine with the cornmeal, salt, black pepper and pickles in a bowl and mix well. Stir in the eggs. For spicy hush puppies, add hot sauce and paprika.

Heat the peanut oil in a deep fryer to 375 degrees. Pinch off pieces of dough, roll into 1-inch balls and deep-fry in batches of 5 to 7 for 3 minutes. Drain on paper towels.

Robert A. Goodman, Westerville, Ohio

White Castles have been enjoyed on every continent, including Antarctica! In 1992, Ernest L. Meyer enjoyed piping hot White Castles at the South Pole. He had brought them all the way from St. Louis.

Mincemeat Apple Cobbler

10 White Castle hamburgers, no pickles, cut into small pieces
5 cups sliced peeled apples
3/4 cup sugar
2 tablespoons all-purpose flour
1/2 teaspoon cinnamon
1/4 teaspoon salt
1 teaspoon vanilla extract

1 tablespoon margarine
1/2 cup flour
1/2 cup sugar
1/2 teaspoon baking powder
1/4 teaspoon salt
2 tablespoons margarine
1 egg, slightly beaten

Preheat the oven to 375 degrees. Grease a 9-inch square baking dish. Combine the hamburgers, apples, 3/4 cup sugar, 2 tablespoons flour, the cinnamon, 1/4 teaspoon salt, the vanilla and 1 tablespoon margarine in a large bowl and mix well. Spoon into the baking dish.

Combine 1/2 cup flour, 1/2 cup sugar, the baking powder, 1/4 teaspoon salt, 2 tablespoons margarine, and the egg with a mixer or pastry blender and mix well. Drop by spoonfuls on top of the mincemeat apple filling. Bake for 35 to 40 minutes or until browned.

Lavina Eich, Minneapolis, Minnesota

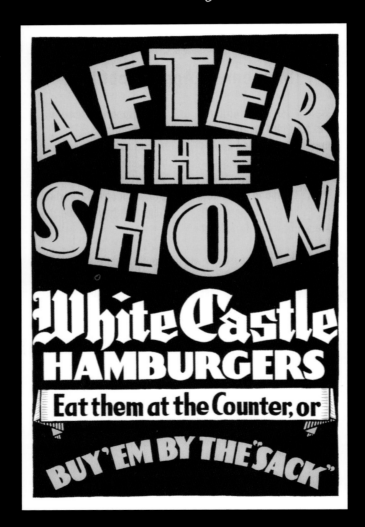

AFTER THE SHOW

White Castle HAMBURGERS

Eat them at the Counter, or

BUY 'EM BY THE "SACK"

*The year is 1970. The scenario…same as last Friday night
and the one before that: I'm getting dressed to go "cruising" with my best friend, Joanie.
Driving around, having a few laughs, looking for boys. Sounds like fun, doesn't it?
I was single, carefree, and it was the '70s for goodness' sake.*

*I hated every minute of it! I am a homebody and always was. I liked being home on a Friday night,
imagining myself in a little house in the suburbs, white picket fence and Mr. Right helping me raise our children.*

*The one bright spot of these evenings was that I knew we would end the night at the Castle, hanging out and
stuffing ourselves with those tasty little burgers, but this night seemed different. Something in the air.
As we pulled into the crowded parking lot, out of the corner of my eye, I spotted a hot rod.
Just another car crammed full with guys, I thought to myself.*

*As we parked our car, I noticed the passenger side of their car open and out stepped this tall, handsome guy with
a thick head of blond hair. He walked past us with an air of confidence and maturity. Was I staring? I'm sure
I was. Suddenly he turned around and headed straight for our car. My friend Joanie (never one to mince words)
started a conversation. I could tell he was younger than I originally thought he was. "No, this one will not want
to settle down anytime soon," I thought to myself. So we locked eyes and then went our separate ways.*

*The Friday night trips to White Castle continued. Some nights I would see the hot rod, other nights I would hold
my breath…no hot rod. I was twenty-two and needed a break from the scene, so I was at the point of telling my
friend "no more Friday nights." As we pulled out of the parking lot that night, I noticed the hot rod pulling in.
I fought the urge to ask Joanie to turn around. Call it fate or timing, but I was just too tired to try again.*

*As we approached home, we saw headlights following us in the dark. We heard a horn blowing
frantically. It was the hot rod urging us to pull over. We did and rolled down the windows slightly.
The young man got out of the car and ran to my side of the car and looked into my window.
Hurriedly, he said, "Hi, my name is Darrell. Will you go out with me?"*

*I send this after Darrell, my husband of 33 years, and I have finished sharing a bag
of White Castles with our granddaughters.*

—Gail Davis, Cincinnati, Ohio

Speedy "King of the Castle" Soup

10 White Castle hamburgers, no ketchup, no mustard
2 envelopes dry onion soup mix

Remove the buns from the hamburgers and reserve the pickles. Cut the hamburgers into quarters.

Prepare the soup according to the package directions. Add the meat and simmer for 20 minutes.

Meanwhile, toast the buns and cut them into croutons. Add the croutons to the soup as desired. Serve with a side salad topped with the reserved pickles. Pour a burgundy wine with the meal. Makes 6 to 8 servings.

Ron Patterson, Oak Forest, Illinois

"What a Surprise" Onion Soup

4 cups thinly sliced onions
3 tablespoons butter
1 garlic clove, minced
3 tablespoons minced fresh parsley
6 cups good-quality beef broth
1/4 cup grated Parmesan cheese
Salt and pepper to taste
10 White Castle hamburgers
5 slices Swiss cheese, cut into halves
5 slices Provolone cheese, cut into halves

Sauté the onions in the butter in a soup pan until dark brown. Stir in the garlic, parsley, beef broth, Parmesan cheese, salt and pepper. Heat to boiling, stirring occasionally. Place each hamburger in an ovenproof bowl. Ladle in the soup. Cover the top of each bowl with cheese, using both types. Place the bowls under the broiler to melt and lightly brown the cheese. Makes 10 servings.

TerryAnn Moore, Oaklyn, New Jersey

Chateau Blanc French Onion Soup

10 White Castle hamburgers, no pickles
4 tablespoons butter or margarine
4 large onions, thinly sliced
1/2 teaspoon sugar
4 (14-ounce) cans beef broth
1 cup shredded Swiss or Gruyère cheese
1/4 cup grated Parmesan cheese

Preheat the oven to 450 degrees. Separate the hamburgers from the buns. Chop the hamburgers finely. Heat the butter in a soup pan and cook the onions, sugar and hamburgers over medium heat for 15 minutes or until the onions are soft, stirring frequently. Add the beef broth and simmer for 10 minutes. Meanwhile, toast the buns. Place a top or bottom bun in a soup bowl or ramekin and place the bowls on a baking sheet. Fill the bowls 3/4 full with the hot soup. Top each with another bun. Sprinkle the cheeses generously over the buns. Bake for 10 minutes or until the cheese is melted and lightly browned.

Marie Gowan, North Vernon, Indiana

Brew-Pub Cheese and Beer Soup

3 tablespoons butter
1/3 cup chopped onion
1/3 cup sliced celery
3 tablespoons all-purpose flour
3/4 teaspoon cayenne pepper
1/2 teaspoon dry mustard
1 1/2 cups milk
2 cups beer
4 cups shredded cheese
10 White Castle hamburgers, buns discarded, meat chopped into small pieces

Melt the butter in a soup pan over medium heat and sauté the onion and celery until tender. Stir in the flour and cook for 4 minutes or until the flour begins to turn golden, stirring frequently. Add the cayenne pepper and mustard and whisk in the milk and beer. Bring to a boil and stir in the cheese and hamburgers. Simmer until the cheese is melted and the soup is thick. Makes 6 to 8 servings.

Sally Sibthorpe, Madison Heights, Michigan

Woohoo! Ahem. Partners Walter Anderson (left) and Billy Ingram (right) proudly display their most awesome business management tool, DUDE! A Curtis OX-5 Travel Air Biplane, in 1927!

Ahem. With Anderson as pilot, the two traveled easily around their company's territory for firsthand supervision of White Castle's operations.

Spicy Cheeseburger Soup

This recipe was the grand prize winner of the 1999 recipe contest.

10 White Castle hamburgers
1¹/₂ cups water
2 cups cubed potatoes
2 small carrots, grated
1 small onion, chopped
¹/₄ cup chopped green bell pepper
1 jalapeño pepper, seeded and chopped
1 garlic clove, minced

1 tablespoon beef bouillon granules
¹/₂ teaspoon salt
2¹/₂ cups milk, divided
3 tablespoons all-purpose flour
8 ounces processed American cheese, cubed
¹/₄ to 1 teaspoon cayenne pepper (optional)
8 ounces bacon, cooked and crumbled

Remove the hamburgers from the buns. Crumble the meat if frozen or cut into very small pieces if fresh.

Combine the water, potatoes, carrots, onion, bell pepper, jalapeño, garlic, beef bouillon granules and salt in a large saucepan. Bring to a boil and reduce the heat. Cover and simmer for 15 to 20 minutes or until the potatoes are tender. Stir in the meat and 2 cups of the milk. Heat through. Combine the flour and remaining milk and mix until smooth; gradually stir into the soup. Bring to a boil and cook for 2 minutes or until the soup is thick and bubbly, stirring frequently. Reduce the heat and stir in the cheese. Cook until the cheese is melted, stirring constantly. Add the cayenne pepper. Top with the bacon just before serving. Serve with toasted buns.

Carol Miller, Northumberland, New York

White Chili

This recipe won the grand prize in the 1995 White Castle recipe contest.

3 bone-in chicken breasts
10 White Castle cheeseburgers
1 (16-ounce) can great northern beans
1 (16-ounce) can white kidney beans
2 cups chopped white onion
1 cup chopped celery
1 cup chopped yellow bell pepper
1 cup chopped tomato
1/2 teaspoon chili powder

1/2 teaspoon dried cilantro
1/2 teaspoon ground cumin
1/2 teaspoon minced garlic
1/2 teaspoon dried oregano
1/2 teaspoon white pepper
8 tablespoons (1 stick) butter
1 cup each shredded Monterey Jack,
    mozzarella and provolone cheeses
1/2 cup chopped parsley

Cook the chicken in 10 cups water until tender. Remove the chicken and let cool. Debone and chop, reserving the broth. Remove the cheeseburgers and pickles from the buns and cut the meat into small pieces. Toast the buns at 225 degrees until dry and grind or crush to crumbs.

Bring the reserved broth to a simmer and add the cheeseburger pieces, pickles, chopped chicken, beans, onion, celery, bell pepper, tomato and seasonings to the soup and simmer for 1 to 2 hours or until the vegetables are tender and flavors are well blended. Add the butter, cheeses, and bread crumbs just before serving and simmer for 15 to 20 minutes. Ladle into soup bowls and garnish with the parsley.

Stan Nikonowicz, Defiance, Missouri

Taco Salad

5 taco salad shells
Nonstick cooking spray
10 White Castle hamburgers
1 envelope taco seasoning mix
Shredded lettuce
3 chopped tomatoes
1 cup shredded Cheddar cheese
1½ avocados, sliced
⅓ (5 tablespoons) cup sour cream
5 teaspoons sliced black olives

Bake the taco shells according to the package directions. Spray a skillet with cooking spray. Crumble the hamburgers into the skillet. Sauté the meat with the taco seasoning in the skillet over medium heat. To assemble the salads, layer the meat, lettuce, tomatoes, cheese and avocados in the taco salad shells, dividing the ingredients evenly. Top with the sour cream and olives.

Dona A. Tracy, Detroit, Michigan

Ham and Cheese Stacks

10 White Castle cheeseburgers with ketchup/mustard mix, no pickles
7 slices Swiss cheese
3 (8-ounce) packages refrigerated crescent roll dough
8 thin slices smoked ham

Preheat the oven to 375 degrees or the temperature recommended on the crescent roll package. Cut the cheeseburgers into halves and the Swiss cheese slices into strips long enough to cover the tops of the cheeseburgers and slightly overhang the ends.

Separate the dough into rectangles. Press along the perforations to seal and flatten the dough slightly. Cut the rectangle into 2 squares. Place 1 ham slice on each dough square; place 1 cheeseburger half (including the bun) on the ham and top with a Swiss cheese strip. Pull the dough up and over the ham and cheeseburger stack so that it is mostly covered. Some openings are fine. Repeat with the remaining cheeseburger halves, cheese and ham. Place stacks on a baking sheet and bake for 12 minutes or until golden (or follow the directions on the crescent roll package). Cook any extra crescent rolls to serve on the side, if desired. Serve hot. Makes 20 servings.

Thomas C. Roy, Southfield, Michigan

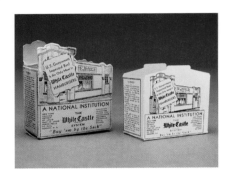

White Hot Brown

10 White Castle hamburgers
4 cups milk
1 teaspoon salt
1/2 teaspoon white pepper
1/2 cup shredded Cheddar cheese
1/2 cup freshly shredded Parmesan cheese
6 tablespoons all-purpose flour
1/2 pound thinly sliced deli roast beef
1 medium tomato, sliced 1/2 inch thick
12 ounces crisp-fried bacon, crumbled

Separate the buns, onions and beef patties. Adjust the oven rack to middle height and turn oven to broil. Arrange the buns on a baking sheet with the cut side up. Broil to a golden brown. Place the buns, cut side up, in a 9x13-inch baking dish. Combine the onions, milk, salt, pepper and cheeses in a saucepan and bring to a boil over low heat. Stir in the flour and cook until thickened, stirring constantly. Layer the roast beef on the buns and top with the beef patties and a tomato slice. Spread the sauce evenly over the beef patties. Broil until golden brown. Remove from the oven and sprinkle with the crumbled bacon.

Tom Phillips, Louisville, Kentucky

Tex-Mex Tasties

10 White Castle hamburgers
1 (16-ounce) can refried beans
1/2 teaspoon dried tarragon
1 (16-ounce) jar chunky salsa
2 tablespoons chopped black olives
1/4 cup shredded Cheddar cheese

Separate the hamburgers from the buns and cut the meat patties diagonally into halves. Spread a thin layer of the refried beans on both halves of the buns. Place a single meat triangle over the beans on each bun. Stir the tarragon into the salsa. Place the buns and meat on a baking sheet. Spoon the salsa mixture, black olives and cheese evenly over the meat patties. Broil until the cheese is melted and the sandwiches are toasted. Makes 20 pieces.

Doris Eberhart, Cincinnati, Ohio

Ladies Who Lunch...at White Castle in furs. The Depression eroded White Castle's working class male customer base, so the company worked to expand sales to women. A company hostess was hired and given the pseudonym "Julia Joyce." Julia brought along scores of hamburgers on social calls to women's clubs and organizations in every White Castle area. (What she really needed was a Crave Case.)

Crescent Loaf

10 White Castle hamburgers
1 (10-ounce) can cream of mushroom soup
1/2 cup milk
3/4 cup finely chopped green bell pepper
1/4 teaspoon black pepper
1 tablespoon Worcestershire sauce
1 (8-count) package crescent roll dough
1/2 cup shredded Cheddar cheese

Preheat the oven to 375 degrees. Tear the hamburgers into small pieces. Mix with the soup, milk, bell pepper, black pepper and Worcestershire sauce in a large bowl. Separate the dough into 2 large rectangles. Overlap the long sides to form a 15x18-inch rectangle. Press the edges and perforations firmly to seal. Spoon about 2 1/2 cups of the hamburger mixture in a 4-inch strip down the center of each rectangle to within 1 inch of ends. Reserve the remaining mixture for topping. Fold the long sides of the dough over the meat toward the center. Bake for 10 to 15 minutes or until golden brown. Spoon the reserved mixture down the center of the partially baked loaf. Sprinkle with the cheese. Bake for 5 minutes longer.

Carla Tosh, Arnold, Missouri

Farmhouse Barbecue Muffins

10 White Castle hamburgers
1 (10-ounce) package refrigerated buttermilk biscuits
1/2 cup ketchup
3 tablespoons brown sugar
1 tablespoon cider vinegar
1/2 teaspoon chili powder
1 cup (4 ounces) shredded Cheddar cheese

Preheat the oven to 375 degrees. Remove the hamburgers from the buns. Crumble the meat if frozen or cut into very small pieces if fresh.

Separate the biscuit dough into 10 biscuits and flatten into 5-inch circles. Press each into the bottom and up the side of a greased muffin cup.

Combine the meat, ketchup, brown sugar, vinegar and chili powder in a small bowl and mix well. Divide the hamburger mixture among the biscuit-lined muffin cups. Sprinkle with the cheese. Bake for 18 minutes or until golden. Cool for 5 minutes before removing from the tins. Serve with toasted buns.

Carol Miller, Northumberland, New York

Burger Pizza

12 White Castle hamburgers
Garlic powder
1 (16-ounce) jar pizza sauce
1 pound shredded mozzarella cheese
Dried oregano
1 (2-ounce) can sliced black olives
1 (4-ounce) can sliced mushrooms
Parmesan cheese

Preheat the oven to 350 degrees. Cut the hamburgers diagonally and separate the buns from the meat. Press the meat and buns into the bottom of a 9x12-inch baking pan to form a pizza "crust." Season with garlic powder. Spread the pizza sauce over the crust and top with the mozzarella cheese and oregano. Layer the black olives and mushrooms over the top and sprinkle with Parmesan cheese. Bake for 20 to 25 minutes or until the cheese is melted and bubbly.

Harold & Joan Sims, Plantation, Florida

Cheeseburger Pizza

10 White Castle hamburgers or cheeseburgers
1 (6-ounce) can tomato sauce
1 small onion, chopped (optional)
1 teaspoon garlic powder
1/2 teaspoon dried basil
6 ounces shredded mozzarella cheese

Preheat the oven to 425 degrees. Oil a medium round pizza pan. Remove the top buns from the hamburgers and set aside. Place the hamburgers and bottom buns in the prepared pizza pan, filling in any gaps with the top buns, cut side up. Cover lightly with the tomato sauce, being careful to not soak the buns. Top with the onion. Sprinkle with the garlic powder, basil and mozzarella cheese. Bake until the cheese is melted and bubbly.

Wendy S. Delmater, Bay Shore, New York

The White Castle Way

I live in a small town in southern Illinois and my closest Craver fix would be quite a drive—to St. Louis or Chicago. Even though I'm far from a White Castle, I still can't deny my Craver ways.

My kitchen walls are a stencilled motif of the White Castle building profile. Previously just the border at the top had the motif, but when White Castle changed its wallpaper, I had no choice but to change mine, too.

My right ankle bears a White Castle tattoo. My license plate displays "wtcstl 1" with a matching White Castle license plate holder, of course. My kitchen cabinets are filled with White Castle memorabilia. I even bought a Chicago jigsaw puzzle, which displays the city's landmarks. Somehow, there were no White Castles on it, but don't worry, I fixed that.

—Michelle Purcell, Mt. Pulaski, Illinois

Stuffed Crust Pizza

10 White Castle hamburgers, no pickles
3 cups shredded mozzarella cheese
1 (14-ounce) can pizza sauce

Preheat the oven to 350 degrees. Remove the top buns from the hamburgers. Place the buns, top side down, on a lightly greased baking sheet with sides touching in 2 rows of 5. Sprinkle with some of the mozzarella cheese. Place the hamburgers on the bottom buns on top of these. Spread the pizza sauce and sprinkle with the remaining cheese. Heat the hamburgers for 15 minutes or until the cheese is bubbly.

Penny Foster, Michigan City, Indiana

Late night Cravers. Business remained steady during the World War II, despite shortages of beef and of sugar for coffee and ketchup. Instead of burgers, the company sold baked beans and coleslaw, which were popular, as were hotdogs and egg sandwiches. French fries sold well at first but dropped off the menu, only to return in the late 1950s.

castle-ified veggies

We are the CADS! The Clifton Adult Delinquent Society.

On the corner of Main Street and Piaget Avenue in Clifton, New Jersey, resides OUR White Castle, our Mecca since the late 1950s. Even though we now live on Long Island, in Florida, Massachusetts, Maryland, and New Jersey, the Castle is a beacon that still calls to us with its siren song. We are the class of 1962 graduates of Clifton High School and the following are examples of our loyalty and devotion.

1. We have stationery (for internal use only, of course) bearing the Clifton High School colors (maroon and gray) but with homage to the White Castle tower.

2. Some years ago, our Castle was torn down and rebuilt. We each own and keep a piece of the original foundation under glass.

3. Two of our crew (Coot and Huey) were members of the Clifton cross-country team. Practice consisted of two laps of the course (approximately one and one-quarter miles each lap), passing the White Castle each time. Many were the days when our two finest would drop off during lap one, scarf up a half dozen and finish lap two with the team!

4. A few years ago the CADS made a pilgrimage to Milwaukee and Chicago to see baseball at Milwaukee County Stadium and Wrigley Field. As we approached Wrigley, there on our left was a White Castle! We ordered our bus driver to pull in.

5. Five of the CADS and three CADETTES (our wives) play golf. Those eight, plus all other senior CAD personnel, possess logoed hats, shirts, golf towels, etc.

6. Today there are 18 CADLINGS (kids) and it is not like the old days: they all use the "new math" — dollars and cents. In our day, we would turn to Huey and ask, "How much money do you have?" He would empty his pockets, stare at the change in his hand, and say, "Six White Castles!"

Each summer we gather to renew old memories and make some new ones. Nearly always, White Castle is in the midst of this annual reunion. We know this entreaty is a bit long, but as you can see, we adopted you long before the Hall of Fame was created. We have always craved you!

Continually Craving,

THE CLIFTON ADULT DELINQUENT SOCIETY:

Richard "Coot" Cattani, Kenneth "Mick" Donnelly, Dr. Jeffrey "Grotmo" Grotsky, Robert "Fax-man" Havasy, Thomas "Emmett" Jordan, Bill "Lips" Lemke, Michael "Long Putts" Libin, Thomas "Huey" Menegus, ED. Miedema, Dennis "Eel" Podolack

Cheesy Broccoli Burger Dish

10 White Castle hamburgers
4 (10-ounce) packages frozen chopped broccoli
1 (1-pound) box Velveeta
1 sleeve round butter crackers, crushed
4 tablespoons butter, melted

Preheat the oven to 350 degrees. Arrange the hamburgers in a large baking dish. Cook the broccoli according to the package directions. Drain and layer over the hamburgers.

Cook the Velveeta in a saucepan over low heat (or microwave in a microwave-safe bowl) until melted. Pour over the broccoli layer. Combine the cracker crumbs and butter in a bowl and mix well. Sprinkle over the layers. Bake for 30 minutes or until the top starts to brown.

Carol Cox, Cincinnati, Ohio

Asparagus Melt

10 White Castle hamburgers, no pickles
8 ounces fresh asparagus, chopped
1 1/4 cups heavy cream
1/4 teaspoon ground allspice
Dash of nutmeg
1/2 teaspoon black pepper
1 teaspoon sugar
Crushed crackers
1/2 cup shredded Swiss cheese

Preheat the oven to 350 degrees. Arrange the hamburgers in a large baking dish. Steam the asparagus until tender; drain. Combine with the cream, allspice, nutmeg, black pepper and sugar and mix well. Spread over the hamburgers and top with the cheese and crushed crackers. Bake for 30 minutes or until the top starts to brown.

Kevin Jude, St. Louis, Missouri

Love it to Smithereens

*My best friend, Jim Babjak, and I wrote a song called "White Castle Blues" in 1977.
As luck would have it, Jim went on to become the lead guitarist for the rock group the Smithereens.
In 1986, the song appeared on the band's first album, Especially for You. The album sold more than
500,000 copies and I am the proud owner of a gold record for my contribution to White Castle lore.*

—*Bob Banta, Fort Collins, Colorado*

Broccoli Bake

10 White Castle hamburgers
2 cups cooked macaroni
2 cups chopped steamed broccoli
1 (10-ounce) can cream of broccoli soup
1 soup can of milk
2 cups shredded Cheddar cheese
3/4 cup grated Parmesan cheese
White Castle onion rings or chips

Preheat the oven to 350 degrees. Arrange the hamburgers in a greased
9x12-inch baking dish. Spread the macaroni over the hamburgers
and add a layer of broccoli. Combine the soup and milk and pour over
the broccoli. Top with the Cheddar cheese and sprinkle with the
Parmesan cheese. Bake until the casserole is hot and the cheeses are
melted. Top with the onion rings or chips and serve.

Karen Knight-Wilburn, Louisville, Kentucky

Customers were plentiful, but shortages of employees and supplies were a fact of life during wartime. Ingram echoed a common joke in his "General Letter of 1943," when *he wrote "If we had some ham, we could have some ham and eggs. If we had some eggs. If we had enough help we could do a good business. If we had something to sell."*

Yucatan Burger 'n' Eggplant Bake

10 White Castle hamburgers, fresh or thawed
1 teaspoon garlic salt
1 teaspoon coarsely ground black pepper
1 medium eggplant, 8 to 9 inches, trimmed
Salt and black pepper to taste
1/4 cup all-purpose flour
2 tablespoons yellow cornmeal
1/4 cup olive oil

1 (15-ounce) can diced tomatoes, undrained
1 (12-ounce) jar chunky salsa
1 teaspoon dried oregano, divided
2 tablespoons grated Parmesan cheese, divided
2 cups (8 ounces) shredded Cheddar or
   mozzarella cheese
8 pitted black olives, quartered

Season the hamburgers on both sides with the garlic salt and black pepper, reserving 2 hamburgers. Brown the remaining 8 hamburgers in a large skillet over medium heat for 8 to 12 minutes, turning once. Remove from the skillet and set aside.

Cut the eggplant lengthwise into 8 thick slices and season with salt and pepper. Combine the flour and cornmeal in a bowl and mix well. Coat the eggplant slices in the flour mixture. Heat the olive oil in a large skillet and brown the eggplant slices on both sides. Arrange 4 eggplant slices per dish in two 8x12-inch baking dishes. Top each eggplant slice with a browned hamburger.

Preheat the oven to 325 degrees. Crumble the remaining 2 hamburgers into the skillet. Brown in the pan drippings for 3 to 4 minutes; drain. Add the undrained tomatoes and salsa; cook just until hot, stirring occasionally. Spoon half of the sauce over the hamburgers in each dish. Sprinkle the oregano and Parmesan cheese over each dish. Top each with the Cheddar cheese and dot with the olives. Bake for 25 to 30 minutes. Note: The cooled casseroles can be wrapped securely and frozen for later use. Makes 8 generous servings.

Michael Cummings, Miami, Florida

A New Kind of Castle in Scotland

In the summer of 1991, I was stationed in Holy Lock, Scotland, repairing submarines for the U.S. Navy. My sister Colleen came to visit and brought along a little something special.

Colleen had put 25 frozen cheeseburgers in a small cooler, which she had then put inside her suitcase. She then smuggled them to me, escorting the Slyders from Detroit to Glasgow. I don't know if I ever asked her what she said when Customs asked whether she had anything to declare. Some things you just don't want to know.

I had some cheeseburgers the day she arrived. She was kind enough not to eat any, knowing what a treat they were for me. The next day, I took some of the remaining Slyders to the ship, where some lucky coworkers and I polished them off. The smell of those steam-grilled burgers wafted throughout our ship. Many people stopped by our shop and commented that it smelled like White Castle. A few select people got a delicious cheeseburger, but most got only the scent and an assurance that any cheeseburgers were just their imagination. Now it can be told: Yes, there were White Castles on the USS Simon Lake and they were better than you remembered!

For the above, I feel Colleen Kish should receive the highest award a civilian can get from White Castle: Entrance into the Craver's Hall of Fame.

—Dan Mack, proud sibling of Colleen Kish, Warren, Michigan

To supply itself with the softest buns imaginable, White Castle opened its second bakery in Newark, N.J., in 1935.

(The first one, in St. Louis, opened earlier the same year.) It was replaced in 1971 by the Carteret, New Jersey, facility.

There is one White Castle for every 764,705.88 people in the United States.

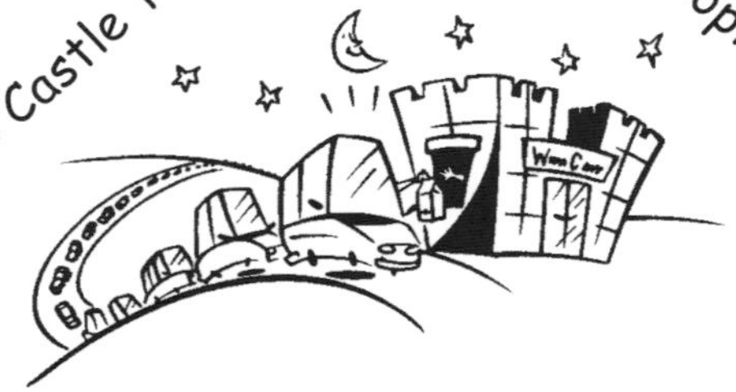

Stuffed Peppers for a Crowd

10 White Castle hamburgers
10 large green bell peppers
1/2 cup chopped onion
1 tablespoon vegetable oil
1 cup cooked rice
1/4 teaspoon garlic powder
2 (15-ounce) cans tomato sauce
8 ounces shredded mozzarella cheese

Preheat the oven to 350 degrees. Cut the hamburgers into quarters. Cut a thin slice from the stem end of each bell pepper, removing the seeds. Lower into boiling water and cook for 5 minutes; drain. Cook the onion in the oil in a large skillet over medium-high heat until tender. Add the rice, garlic powder and tomato sauce and mix well.

Arrange the bell peppers upright in a 9x13-inch baking dish. Stuff 4 hamburger quarters into each bell pepper. Pour the tomato mixture over the bell peppers and top with the cheese. Bake, uncovered, for 30 to 45 minutes or until cheese is golden brown.
Makes 10 servings.

Arlene Hlad, Burbank, Illinois

This White Castle advertisement targeted women and emphasized the wholesomeness of the restaurant's ground beef. White Castle's advertisements frequently included discount coupons. These "sales" brought in "huge deluges of people," said one operator, and the stores hired relief employees to handle the crowds. (Note that the ad, circa 1931, offers delivery service of 50 or more Slyders anytime between 6 a.m. and 6 p.m.— the first Craver catering!)

Fried Stuffed Peppers

10 White Castle hamburgers
8 medium bell peppers
1/2 cup all-purpose flour
7 egg whites
7 egg yolks, beaten
Vegetable oil for frying

Crumble the hamburgers. Roast the bell peppers until the skins are brown. Place the peppers in a paper bag and let stand for 10 to 15 minutes. Remove the skins and cut a slit in each bell pepper. Remove the seeds but leave the stems. Stuff the bell peppers with the crumbled hamburgers and coat with flour.

Beat the egg whites in a bowl until stiff. Fold the egg yolks gently into the egg whites.

Heat the oil in a large skillet. Dip the bell peppers in the egg mixture and fry in the hot oil until golden brown, turning occasionally.

Rose Bribiesca, East Chicago, Indiana

Castle-Stuffed Potatoes

*This recipe won the grand prize in the
1998 recipe contest.*

5 large baking potatoes, baked, cut into halves
8 ounces sour cream
1 teaspoon salt
1/2 teaspoon black pepper
10 White Castle hamburgers, no pickles
1 medium green bell pepper, finely chopped
1 medium onion, finely chopped
1 tablespoon margarine
1 1/2 cups shredded Cheddar cheese
4 tablespoons chives

Scoop most of the pulp from the potatoes into a bowl,
leaving a shell. Add the sour cream, salt and black
pepper and mix well. Cut the hamburgers into small
pieces and place in a bowl. Sauté the bell pepper and
onion in the margarine and stir into the potato
mixture. Spoon into the potato skins, filling over the
top. Sprinkle with the cheese and chives. Bake at
325 degrees for 35 to 45 minutes or until the cheese
is melted. Makes 10 servings.

Joy Bandemer, Bolingbrook, Illinois

Cool Taco Salad

10 White Castle hamburgers
2 tablespoons vegetable oil
1/4 teaspoon garlic powder
1 envelope taco seasoning mix
1 head lettuce, shredded
2 medium tomatoes, chopped
Sour cream
Chopped green onions

Remove the buns from the hamburgers and chop.
Sauté in the oil in a skillet to make croutons.
Sprinkle with the garlic powder.

Chop the hamburger patties and combine with
the taco seasoning. Cook according to the
package directions. Place the lettuce on a large
platter. Top with the meat mixture and tomatoes.
Garnish with sour cream, green onions
and the croutons.

Arlene Hlad, Burbank, Illinois

White Castle began using all vegetable oil in 1965, and continues to use it to this day.

Hot Castle Potato Salad

10 White Castle hamburgers, no pickles
5 medium red potatoes
8 to 10 slices bacon,
cooked crisp and crumbled
1 to 2 green onions, finely chopped
2 celery stalks, finely chopped
1/2 cup mayonnaise

1/4 cup vinegar
2 teaspoons sugar
2 teaspoons salt
1/2 teaspoon black pepper
1 teaspoon mustard
Sour cream (optional)

Separate the hamburger meat from the buns. Chop the meat. Boil the potatoes in salted water to cover in a saucepan until tender; drain and cool. Cut the potatoes into slices. Combine with the meat, bacon, green onions and celery in a large bowl and mix well.

Preheat the oven to 375 degrees. Combine the mayonnaise, vinegar, sugar, salt, black pepper and mustard in a bowl. Pour over the potato mixture and mix well. Spoon the mixture into a baking dish and bake for 20 minutes. Serve hot with a dollop of sour cream. Serve with toasted buttered buns.

Phyllis Cantrell, Louisville, Kentucky

Pretty Far Piece

I grew up in Cincinnati, Ohio, went through college there, and left at 21, some forty-two years ago. As a young man, I visited the White Castle near my home at least twice a week, never realizing that I had developed the Crave for those burgers.

Now that I don't live anywhere near a White Castle, I drive from my home in Georgia to Nashville, Tennessee, a five-hour drive, at least once a month just to have lunch at White Castle. I've tallied the dates on my old calendars: During the past 10 years, I have made 290 trips just for a White Castle!

—David Silvian, Bogart, Georgia

Garden Casserole

10 White Castle hamburgers or cheeseburgers
2 medium tomatoes, thinly sliced
3/4 cup chopped green bell pepper
3/4 cup sour cream
1/2 cup mayonnaise
3/4 cup shredded sharp Cheddar cheese
2 tablespoons chopped onion
Paprika (optional)

Preheat the oven to 375 degrees. Arrange 8 hamburgers upside down in a greased 8x11-inch baking dish. Cut the remaining 2 hamburgers into halves and fill in the spaces. Layer the tomatoes and bell pepper over the hamburgers. Combine the sour cream, mayonnaise, cheese and onion. Spoon the mixture over the vegetables. Sprinkle with paprika. Bake for 25 to 30 minutes or until hot and bubbly. Makes 6 to 8 servings.

Monica Steinbis, Vevay, Indiana

Three packets of ketchup have the nutritional value of a single ripe tomato.

Tomato and Pepper Bake

10 White Castle hamburgers with pickles
4 large green bell peppers
4 large tomatoes
1/2 cup (1 stick) butter
10 garlic cloves, minced
12 ounces fresh mushrooms, stems removed, sliced

1 1/2 cups white rice
1 (10-ounce) box chopped frozen spinach, thawed and drained
1/2 teaspoon salt
1/2 teaspoon white pepper
1 cup Parmesan cheese

Preheat the oven to 350 degrees. Separate the hamburger patties from the buns. Process the buns in a food processor until fine crumbs form. Chop the hamburger patties into bite-size pieces. Cut off the tops of the bell peppers, removing the cores and seeds. Scoop out the tomato pulp to form shells, reserving the pulp.

Heat the butter in a large skillet and sauté the garlic and mushrooms until tender.
Stir in the chopped meat patties and bun crumbs.

Prepare the rice according to the package directions, adding the reserved tomato pulp, spinach, salt and white pepper. Cook over medium heat. Combine the rice and meat mixtures and mix well. Stuff the bell peppers and tomatoes with the mixture. Top with the Parmesan cheese. Place the tomatoes and peppers in a deep baking dish and bake for 30 minutes or until the tomatoes and peppers are tender.

Jill Conkwright, Niles, Ohio

Burger and Zucchini Casserole

10 White Castle hamburgers with onions
2 to 3 small zucchini, cut into 1/4-inch slices
1/4 cup all-purpose flour
8 ounces meatless spaghetti sauce
8 ounces ricotta cheese

1 egg
Grated Parmesan cheese
8 tablespoons butter
1/4 teaspoon garlic powder

Preheat the oven to 350 degrees. Remove the hamburgers from the buns. Arrange the zucchini slices
in a greased 8-inch baking dish. Sprinkle with the flour. Top with the hamburgers
and onions. Spread the spaghetti sauce over the hamburgers.

Beat the ricotta cheese and egg in a bowl and spread over the spaghetti sauce. Sprinkle with Parmesan cheese.
Bake, uncovered, for 30 minutes or microwave on HIGH for 10 minutes. Let stand for 10 minutes.

Combine the butter and garlic powder in a bowl and spread over the buns.
Broil the buns until toasted. Serve the casserole on the buns.

Marilyn Wagner, Columbus, Ohio

Ahh, a moment's peace....opening day at a White Castle in 1945 is   *deceptively quiet, but the customers will soon fix that.*

Zucchini Ripieni

10 White Castle hamburgers
6 medium zucchini
$^1/_4$ cup olive oil
1 tablespoon minced garlic
$^1/_4$ cup chopped prosciutto
2 tablespoons tomato paste

1 egg, beaten
$^1/_2$ cup freshly shredded Parmesan cheese
2 tablespoons chopped fresh oregano, or
   1 teaspoon dried oregano, crumbled
Butter

Chop the hamburgers. Cut the zucchini lengthwise into halves. Scoop out most of the pulp, leaving a $^1/_4$-inch-thick shell. Coarsely chop the zucchini pulp and reserve.

Heat the olive oil in a skillet over medium heat and sauté the garlic and reserved zucchini pulp for 5 minutes; drain well. Let cool slightly and combine with the chopped hamburgers, prosciutto, tomato paste, egg, most of the Parmesan cheese and the oregano. Reserve some of the Parmesan cheese for later use.

Preheat the oven to 375 degrees. Arrange the zucchini shells in a greased baking dish. Stuff the shells with the filling mixture. Sprinkle with the reserved Parmesan cheese and dot with butter.

Bake for 30 minutes or until the filling is tender and lightly browned but not mushy. Cover with foil if the filling seems to be overbrowning.

Lori Piecuch. Lenox, Illinois

dinner in a parallel universe

We've been cravin' on the railroads

Working in the railroad supply industry, we often need to do
field tests across our country's rails. While testing in Indiana one morning,
one of our engineers was assigned to bring the doughnuts for the day.
He got the Crave and brought his own brand of delicacy—Slyders by the sack!

This went over so well that we took up a collection the next year to repeat this
momentous event. When all the Slyders were bought and eaten, we found
that we had an embarrassing amount of money left over. We donated that amount
to a local charity, and so was born our annual Slyder Charity Breakfast Boo-Fay.

For fourteen years, we've re-enacted this event at work, and this year
we purchased twenty-five hundred Slyders from our local White Castle in Countryside, Illinois;
of course, they were hot and ready for our 7 a.m. festivities!

This time, the extra money we collected totaled almost $6000,
which went to a needy charity in our area.

Over the years, we've consumed more than twenty thousand Slyders and have
collected about $40,000 for donation to charity!

—Craig Prudian, Willowbrook, Illinois

Every year, the speediest White Castle griddle operators take part in the Fastest Griddle Contest at the home office in Columbus, Ohio. Contestants are timed setting up the griddle, removing the burgers from the griddle, and sacking 30 burgers.

Castles Roma

10 White Castle hamburgers
16 ounces cottage cheese
1 (10-ounce) package frozen chopped spinach,
thawed and squeezed dry
1 (25-ounce) jar spaghetti sauce
1/2 cup grated Parmesan cheese
2 cups shredded mozzarella cheese

Preheat the oven to 350 degrees. Place 5 hamburgers in a Dutch oven. Top with a layer of half the cottage cheese and half the spinach. Pour half the spaghetti sauce over the top. Sprinkle with 1/4 cup of the Parmesan cheese and 1 cup of the mozzarella cheese. Repeat the layers. Bake for 30 minutes.

Juanita Helton, Bloomington, Illinois

Open-Face Castles

10 White Castle hamburgers, no pickles
2 packages brown gravy mix
1/2 envelope dry onion soup mix
5 cups prepared instant mashed potatoes

Cut the hamburgers diagonally into halves and arrange 4 halves on a plate with a space in the center.

Prepare the gravy mix according to the package directions; add the onion soup mix and simmer for 5 minutes. Spoon 1 cup of the mashed potatoes into the space in the middle of the hamburgers. Ladle gravy over the top. Serve with the remaining mashed potatoes and gravy. Makes 5 servings.

Kathy Brandon, Monticello, Indiana

Awesome Italian-Style Pizza Burgers

10 White Castle hamburgers
3 oval slices provolone cheese
$^1/_2$ cup tomato-based pasta sauce
$^1/_4$ cup diced onion
$^1/_4$ cup diced green bell pepper
$^1/_4$ cup shredded mozzarella cheese

Preheat the oven to 350 degrees. Remove top buns from the hamburgers and set aside. Arrange the hamburgers in a greased deep baking dish. Stack the provolone cheese and cut into squares to fit the hamburgers. Place the cheese on the hamburgers. Spread the pasta sauce over the provolone cheese. Layer with the onion and bell pepper. Sprinkle with the mozzarella cheese. Bake for 8 to 10 minutes. Remove from the oven and cut the hamburgers apart. Replace the top buns.

Jocelyn Williams, Park Forest, Illinois

Burger Boats

6 medium baking potatoes
10 White Castle hamburgers
6 tablespoons butter or margarine, softened
$^1/_2$ cup sour cream
$^1/_4$ cup milk
6 slices bacon, crisp-fried and crumbled, divided
$^1/_2$ cup shredded Cheddar cheese
$^1/_2$ cup grated Parmesan cheese
4 green onions, sliced

Preheat the oven to 350 degrees. Bake the potatoes for 1 hour or until tender when gently pressed. Remove from the oven. Increase the oven temperature to 400 degrees. Chop the hamburgers finely and combine with the butter, sour cream, milk, half the bacon, the cheeses and green onions in a large bowl and mix well. Cut the top quarter from each potato and scoop out the pulp, forming a shell. Stuff the hamburger mixture into the shells. Top with the remaining bacon. Place on a baking sheet. Bake for 20 to 30 minutes or until the tops are light brown and the potatoes are hot.

Candy Barnhart, Hollywood, California

*O*perators wore paper caps manufactured by White Castle's incorporated subsidiary, Paperlynen Company, located on the site of the existing home office in Columbus, Ohio. It was the company's original idea to

manufacture paper caps for operators. Paperlynen began formal production in 1932 and sold paper caps to retail outlets, and in later years, to most of White Castle's competition. They ceased operations in 1976.

10 White Castle Barbecue Beef Casserole

10 White Castle hamburgers
1 cup barbecue sauce
4 cups prepared instant mashed potatoes
1 cup (4 ounces) shredded sharp Cheddar cheese
1 cup whipping cream, whipped

Preheat the oven to 350 degrees. Remove the top buns from the hamburgers. Arrange the hamburgers in a greased 9x13-inch baking dish. Spread with the barbecue sauce. Replace the top buns. Cover the hamburgers evenly with the mashed potatoes. Fold the cheese into the whipped cream and spread over the potatoes. Bake for 30 to 35 minutes or until the cheese is golden brown.

Carol Krueger, Hickory Hills, Illinois

Firehouse Beans & Castles

1¹/₂ pounds hot Italian sausage, casings removed
1¹/₂ pounds ground beef
1 bunch green onions, chopped
1 green bell pepper, chopped
1 large onion, chopped
3 garlic cloves, minced
2 (28-ounce) cans baked beans
2 (15-ounce) cans hot chili beans
5 tablespoons horseradish

3 tablespoons paprika
Salt and pepper to taste
1 (11-ounce) jar jalapeño peppers with juice
1 cup brown sugar
10 ounces ketchup
Hot pepper sauce to taste
10 White Castle hamburgers
Sour cream
2 cups shredded Cheddar cheese

Preheat the oven to 325 degrees. Brown the sausage and ground beef with the green onions,
bell pepper, onion and garlic in a large skillet over medium-high heat. Combine the meat mixture with the beans,
horseradish, paprika, salt, pepper, jalapeños, brown sugar, ketchup and hot sauce in a large bowl. Spoon into a
baking dish and bake for 1 hour. Place 2 hamburgers on each plate and top with the
ground beef mixture. Serve with sour cream and the cheese. Makes 5 servings.

Kevin Connell, Marc Kleinline and Steve Treinish, Columbus, Ohio

A Balanced Meal
For Growing Bodies

White Castle
HAMBURGERS
"BUY 'EM BY THE SACK"

Burger Pot Pie

1/3 cup (5 tablespoons) margarine or butter
1/3 cup all-purpose flour
1/3 cup chopped onion
1/2 teaspoon salt
1/4 teaspoon black pepper
13/4 cups beef broth
2/3 cup milk
1 (10-ounce) package frozen peas and
carrots, thawed
10 White Castle hamburgers

Preheat the oven to 425 degrees. Melt the margarine in a 2-quart saucepan over medium heat.
Stir in the flour, onion, salt and pepper. Cook until the mixture bubbles, stirring constantly. Remove from the
heat and stir in the broth and milk. Bring to a boil, stirring constantly. Cook for 1 minute, stirring constantly. Add the
peas and carrots and mix well. Remove the buns from the hamburgers and set aside. Crumble the hamburgers.
Stir into the sauce mixture. Place the bottom buns in a lightly greased 9x9-inch pan. Pour the sauce mixture
over the buns. Top with the top buns. Bake for 35 minutes or until golden brown.

Serena Booker, Roxana, Illinois

The Mechling family of Wichita, Kansas, enjoying burgers at home, early 1930s. Once the Great Depression caused widespread industrial layoffs and impoverished many in the working class, marketing efforts specifically targeted the middle-class consumer.

Mr. Owen's Leek Pie

10 White Castle hamburgers with pickles and onions
6 tablespoons butter
2 pounds leeks or Bermuda onions, sliced
6 eggs

2 cups sour cream or nonfat plain yogurt
1/2 cup sherry or 1 cup beer
1 teaspoon salt
1/2 teaspoon freshly ground black pepper
1 egg white, slightly beaten

Remove the pickles and chop. Remove the buns from the hamburgers and knead them into dough. Roll with a rolling pin and press into two 9-inch pie plates.

Preheat the oven to 450 degrees. Melt the butter in a saucepan and sauté the leeks and onions from the hamburgers until transparent.

Combine the eggs, sour cream, sherry, salt, black pepper and chopped pickles in a bowl. Stir into the leek mixture. Brush the bottom of the pie shells with the beaten egg white. Fill the shells with the leek mixture. Bake for about 10 minutes. Reduce the heat to 300 degrees and bake for 30 minutes longer or until browned.

Top each pie with 5 hamburgers (to warm without cooking) before removing from the oven.

David Owen, Louisville, Kentucky

Taco Fondue

12 frozen White Castle hamburgers
2 cups grated sharp American cheese
6 eggs
3/4 teaspoon dry mustard
2 1/4 cups milk
1 envelope taco seasoning mix
1 (10-ounce) can cream of mushroom soup
1/2 cup milk

Cover the bottom of a greased 9x13-inch baking dish with the hamburgers. Top with the cheese.

Beat the eggs and mustard in a bowl. Add 2 1/4 cups milk and the taco seasoning mix. Pour over the cheese. Cover the baking dish and refrigerate for at least 8 hours.

Preheat the oven to 300 degrees. Combine the soup with 1/2 cup milk in a bowl and mix well. Pour over the casserole. Bake for 1 1/4 hours.

Marion Kisling, Kingwood, Texas

Crave-Point Average

*I currently attend Lindenwood University in St. Charles, Missouri, and I have a GPA of 3.5.
The nearest Castle is about 1.5 miles down the highway. Prior to Lindenwood I attended the St. Louis
Community College and carried a GPA of 3.9. The nearest Castle was two blocks from my parents' house,
where I resided. Before that, I attended Truman State, where I had a GPA of 2.1, and the nearest Castle
was in St. Louis, more than 190 miles away. Coincidence? I do not think so.*

—Casey Dikkers, Hazelwood, Missouri

Hamburger Lasagna

10 White Castle hamburgers
2 to 3 cups tomato-based pasta sauce
8 ounces sliced fresh mushrooms or
1/4 cup drained canned mushrooms
Butter
8 ounces (2 cups) shredded mozzarella cheese
3 tablespoons grated Parmesan cheese

Preheat the oven to 325 degrees. Grease a baking
dish large enough for 10 hamburgers to fit in 1 layer
with sides touching. Fit the hamburgers into the
baking dish and spoon some of the pasta sauce
over and between the hamburgers. Sauté the
mushrooms in butter. Spread over the hamburgers.
Add a layer of the pasta sauce over all. Top with
the mozzarella cheese and Parmesan cheese.
Bake for 15 to 20 minutes.

Jo Guardino, Staten Island, New York

*Knickers and argyles:
it's as if someone
called Central
Casting for a
1920s to 1930s
Craver Kid.
Note the milk in
individual bottles!*

Using three griddles, most White Castles have a production capacity of 2,000 burgers an hour.

Herb-Roasted Chicken

3/4 cup (1 1/2 sticks) butter
8 ounces smoked sausage, diced
4 celery stalks, diced
1 small garlic clove, minced
10 White Castle hamburgers,
no pickles, chopped
1 tablespoon dried thyme

1 tablespoon dried sage
Salt and pepper to taste
1 bunch fresh thyme, chopped
1 bunch fresh sage, chopped
1 (5 to 6-pound) roasting chicken
1 large onion, thickly sliced

Melt 1/2 cup of the butter in a large skillet and brown the sausage. Add the celery and sauté for 90 seconds or until tender-crisp. Add the garlic, hamburgers, dried thyme and dried sage and sauté until heated through. Season with salt and pepper to taste. Let stand to cool.

Preheat the oven to 325 degrees. Combine the fresh thyme and sage in a bowl. Loosen the skin of the chicken and insert the fresh herbs under the skin. Stuff the chicken cavity with the hamburger mixture, reserving any excess stuffing in a small casserole.

Line a roasting pan with the onion slices. Arrange the chicken on the onion. Season the chicken with salt and pepper and dot with the remaining 1/4 cup butter. Roast for 1 3/4 hours to 2 1/2 hours or until a meat thermometer inserted into the white meat registers 180 degrees and the juices run clear when the drumsticks are pierced with a knife, basting occasionally. Let stand for 15 minutes before carving. Bake any remaining stuffing (at the same time as the chicken) for 45 minutes.

Andrew Tweddle, Warren, Michigan

The Castle's Secret Ammo

This recipe was the grand prize winner in the 2004 Crave Time Cook Off.

10 White Castle hamburgers
¼ cup herb-flavored oil-pack
sun-dried tomatoes, chopped
1 cup shredded pepper Jack cheese
⅓ cup grated Parmesan cheese
½ teaspoon garlic powder

3 large bell peppers, any color
6 thin slices Cheddar cheese
½ cup sour cream
3 black olives, chopped
Salsa

Grind the hamburgers to crumbs in a food processor. Combine with the sun-dried tomatoes, pepper Jack cheese, Parmesan cheese and garlic powder in a large bowl. Preheat the oven to 350 degrees. Cut the bell peppers into halves lengthwise; remove the stems and seeds. Arrange cut side down on a broiler pan. Broil until the skins are charred; remove and discard the skins. Place the bell pepper halves cut side up in a greased shallow baking dish. Fill with the hamburger mixture. Bake for 20 minutes. Top each bell pepper half with 1 Cheddar cheese slice. Bake for 10 to 20 minutes longer or until tender.

Arrange the bell pepper halves on a serving platter. Top each with a dollop of the sour cream and garnish with the olives. Serve with salsa. Makes 6 servings.

Lois Dowling, Tacoma, Washington

Stuffed Cabbage Rolls

I large cabbage, cored
1/2 cup (1 stick) butter
1 onion, chopped
1/2 cup chopped celery
1/2 cup hot water

10 White Castle hamburgers, chopped
Salt and pepper to taste
1 (10-ounce) can tomato soup
1/2 cup hot water
1/2 teaspoon oregano

*T*he all-night hours of White Castle made it attractive for
late shift workers, overnight travelers, and night owls, as
it was often the only source of a hot meal at that hour.
Note the building's signature stained glass window inserts.

Boil the cabbage in water to cover in a large saucepan
for 15 minutes or until the leaves become pliable.
Remove 6 large leaves; reserve remaining
cabbage for another use. Preheat the oven to 350
degrees. Melt the butter in a large skillet and sauté the
onion and celery until transparent. Add 1/2 cup hot
water, the hamburgers, salt and pepper.

Divide the mixture among the cabbage leaves. Roll the
leaves to enclose the filling, tucking in the ends and
securing with toothpicks. Arrange the rolls in a
baking dish. Mix the tomato soup with 1/2 cup hot water
and the oregano and pour over the rolls. Bake, covered,
for 11/2 hours or until the cabbage is tender.
Makes 6 servings.

Joan Willy, St. Paul, Minnesota

A Steamy Proposal

My husband Stefan and I dated through college, each living at home with our parents and working full-time to pay for tuition and save up money. We always joked about how our idea of a big night out on the town was going to White Castle. Just after Stefan graduated and began his teaching career (we were both still living with our parents), he called to tell me to get dressed up for a special night out.

He showed up in a limo, dressed in his best suit. Much to my surprise, the driver took us straight to White Castle. Stefan escorted me into the restaurant, spread out a linen tablecloth, pulled out a case of flowers, and went to the counter to order.

When he returned to the table, he handed out the food, leaving one burger box in the middle of the table. After we ate, he handed the box to me. I found an engagement ring inside.

Of course, I said "yes" and the whole restaurant, including the employees, went wild! We've been married for more than eleven years—and we still love White Castle burgers!

—Gabrielle and Stefan Farrenkopf, Gahanna, Ohio

Castles Cordon Bleu

10 White Castle hamburgers

4 chicken breast halves

8 thin slices apricot-glazed ham

8 ounces Swiss cheese

Vegetable oil for deep frying

Refrigerate the hamburgers for 8 hours or more. Process 6 of the hamburgers in a food processor to a medium grind. Process 4 of the hamburgers to a fine grind. Pound each chicken breast with a mallet to a 1/4-inch thickness. Layer the ham and cheese slices, 1 at a time, over each chicken breast until all slices are used. Divide the medium-ground hamburgers among the 4 chicken breasts, leaving a 1/4-inch border along the long side. Roll each chicken breast from the short side to enclose the filling. Tuck each end of the roll under. Coat each chicken roll in the finely ground hamburgers. Heat the oil in a deep fryer to 375 degrees. Deep-fry the chicken rolls for 10 minutes per roll or until golden brown. Drain and serve. Makes 4 servings.

Jonathan Skinner, Wilmington, Illinois

When meat rationing ended in 1946, the country was ready for a burger, and sales surged, though the price of a burger had doubled to 10 cents.

Schenck Stuffed Chicken Bordelaise

10 White Castle hamburgers with onions and pickles
1 cup chopped fresh spinach
1 1/2 cups shredded mozzarella cheese
1/4 cup chopped garlic, divided
Salt and black pepper to taste
Melted butter
1/4 cup paprika
4 boneless chicken breast halves with skin
1 egg yolk
1 envelope brown gravy mix

1 large onion, minced
5 carrots, chopped
2 celery stalks, chopped
1 tablespoon bay leaves
1/2 tablespoon dried thyme
2 tablespoons butter
2 tablespoons chopped shallots
3/4 cup Bordeaux wine
2 tablespoons minced parsley
2 tablespoons lemon juice
Cayenne pepper to taste

Preheat the oven to 375 degrees. Remove the buns from the hamburgers. Crumble the hamburgers, onions and pickles into a large bowl. Place the buns, cut side up, on a baking sheet. Add the spinach, mozzarella cheese, half the garlic, salt and black pepper to the hamburger mixture. Brush the buns with melted butter and toast until dry; crumble into a bowl. Stir in the paprika and the remaining garlic.

Stuff 2 tablespoons of the breading mixture under the chicken skin. Brush each chicken breast with the egg yolk and coat with the bun mixture. Bake, uncovered, in a greased baking dish for 45 to 55 minutes. Prepare the gravy mix in a large saucepan according to the package directions. Add the onion, carrots, celery, bay leaves and thyme. Simmer for 10 minutes; set aside. Melt 2 tablespoons butter in a saucepan and sauté the shallots. Add the wine and simmer until reduced by 1/2. Add 1 1/2 cups of the gravy, the parsley, lemon juice, salt, black pepper and cayenne pepper and cook until heated through. Drizzle 1 to 2 tablespoons sauce over each chicken breast.

Maria Schenck, St. Louis, Missouri

Castle Stuffed Pork Chops

1/2 cup milk	12 White Castle hamburgers, no pickles, chopped
1 egg, beaten	4 slices white bread, cubed
6 pork chops	1 teaspoon poultry seasoning
Vegetable oil	1/2 teaspoon black pepper
1 small onion, chopped	2 tablespoons chopped parsley
1 cup chopped celery	1/2 teaspoon salt

Preheat the oven to 350 degrees. Combine the milk and egg in a bowl. Brown the pork chops in hot vegetable oil in a skillet and set aside. Sauté the onion and celery in a skillet until tender; place in a large bowl. Add the hamburgers, bread, poultry seasoning, black pepper, parsley and salt and mix well. Add the egg mixture and mix well.

Place 1 pork chop at 1 end of a greased loaf pan. Spoon 2 large spoonfuls of the stuffing mixture beside the pork chop. Repeat until the 6 pork chops and the stuffing mixture are used. Bake for 1 hour. Serve hot. Make 6 servings.

Joy Bandemer, Bolingbrook, Illinois

Celebrity Picnic

In 1998, I was selected to escort NBC Today Show weatherman Willard Scott to the Ohio Governor's Conference on Aging. At the conclusion of the conference, Willard was presented with three huge insulated containers of White Castle hamburgers.
Willard asked me to place the hamburgers off to the side until we were ready to leave for the airport. As we were leaving the conference, Willard suggested that we take the hamburgers to the airport and figure out what to do with them at the departure gate.

We arrived at the Columbus Airport, where arrangements had been made for us to have a special parking space in the VIP parking area. As we were unloading Willard's bags from the trunk, people began noticing the NBC celebrity and surrounded our car requesting autographs. While signing autographs, Willard turned to me and asked if we had the three boxes of White Castle hamburgers. I said "yes," and Willard then asked the crowd if they wanted a Slyder tailgate party. The crowd roared with enthusiasm and the Slyder party began. We must have handed over 100 White Castle hamburgers to those gathered. Willard waved good-bye to the crowd and made his way to the waiting plane, his pockets stuffed with an assortment of hamburgers.

—Charlie Evranian, New Albany, Ohio

Stuffed Pork Roast

10 White Castle hamburgers, no pickles
1 (16-ounce) package creamed spinach
6 hard-boiled eggs, chopped
1/2 cup chicken broth

1/2 tablespoon salt
3/4 teaspoon black pepper
1 tablespoon garlic powder
4 to 5 pounds pork loin roast, boneless

Preheat the oven to 350 degrees. Tear the hamburgers into pieces. Combine with the spinach, eggs and broth in a bowl. Combine the salt, pepper and garlic powder in a separate bowl. Butterfly the pork roast. Lay the roast flat and spread the hamburger mixture evenly over the top. Starting at 1 end, roll the roast up as tightly as possible and tie with kitchen twine. Rub the spices over the outside of the roast and place seam side down in a roasting pan or roasting bag. Cook for 2 to 31/2 hours. Let stand for 10 minutes; cut the string and slice.

Daniel Orzano, Valley Stream, New York

Experts believe that cucumbers were first pickled in Mesopotamia about 4,500 years ago.

Burmese Curry Cups

10 White Castle hamburgers
2 tablespoons peanut or other oil
2 tablespoons chopped peeled ginger
4 to 5 green onions, sliced
(including 1 inch of green part)
1 tablespoon curry powder
1 large dried red chile, chopped, or
2 teaspoons ground chile

2/3 cup (6 ounces) canned coconut milk
1/2 cup (4 ounces) beef broth
3 tablespoons fish sauce
2 teaspoon sugar
1 cup chopped celery leaves or cilantro
3 limes, cut into quarters

Remove the hamburgers from the buns and cut each bun into 6 pieces. Set the pieces aside and allow to dry for a few hours (or bake them in a 150- to 200-degree oven until dry). Cut the meat patties into quarters and set aside.

Preheat the oven to 325 degrees. Heat a wok and add the peanut oil. Sauté the ginger and green onions until lightly browned; add the curry powder and red chile and mix well. Add the coconut milk and the meat patties and bring to a boil. Reduce the heat and stir in the beef broth. Add the fish sauce and sugar; turn off the heat.

Combine the buns, meat mixture and green onions in a large bowl. Add enough of the wok liquid so the mixture is moist but not soggy. Spoon the meat mixture into individual baking cups or a greased small baking dish. Bake for 25 to 30 minutes. Sprinkle each serving with the celery leaves and serve with a lime quarter.

Ned Omalia, Albuquerque, New Mexico

Little Patsy Mechling of Wichita, Kansas, enjoys a White Castle burger at home. As part of an effort to promote healthy eating of the burgers at home,

White Castle issued menu suggestion pamphlets featuring the burgers as a main dish paired with salads, vegetables, and other side items.

East Indian Bobotie

10 White Castle hamburgers
4 tablespoons butter
2 onions, diced
1 apple, peeled, cored and diced
2 tablespoons curry powder
1 tablespoon sugar
2 eggs
2 tablespoons vinegar
Salt to taste
2 teaspoons freshly ground black pepper

1 teaspoon turmeric
12 slivered almonds (optional)
6 bay leaves
1 cup skim milk
Cooked rice
Condiments: chopped green onions, shredded coconut, raisins, chopped peanuts, chutney, chopped hard-cooked eggs, sliced tomatoes, sliced bell peppers

Remove the hamburgers from the buns. Crumble or chop the meat patties into small pieces. Soak the buns in water and squeeze dry. Tear the buns into small pieces. Brown the hamburgers in 2 tablespoons of the butter in a skillet and set aside.

Preheat the oven to 350 degrees. Sauté the onions and apples in the remaining butter. Mix with the hamburgers, bun pieces, curry powder, sugar, 1 egg, the vinegar, salt, pepper and turmeric. Add the slivered almonds. Spoon the mixture into a greased 9x13-inch baking dish. Add the bay leaves in an upright position. Bake for 30 to 45 minutes.

Beat the remaining egg with the milk and pour over the bobotie about 10 minutes before removing the dish from the oven. Discard the bay leaves before serving. Serve over rice with condiments. As a variation, use apricot jam instead of sugar. Makes 10 servings.

Carol M. Miller, Northumberland, New York

Initially, White Castle stores were nearly all urban, but expansions to the suburbs began early. This location, at 490 Sunrise Highway, Lynbrook, Long Island, is officially called "New York #9."

It had a prime position near (and a scenic view of) the elevated tracks of the Long Island Railroad. It opened September 1933. Opening week's sales were $304.75.

Stuffed Rouladen Weiss Schloss

10 White Castle hamburgers with onions and pickles	8 ounces bacon, cut into 3- to 4-inch strips
1 egg	1 cup all-purpose flour
2^{1}/2 to 3 pounds thinly sliced round steak	2 teaspoons seasoned salt
Bacon drippings or vegetable oil	2 cups water
	1 envelope onion gravy mix

Preheat the oven to 150 degrees. Remove the hamburgers from the buns, placing the bottom buns in the oven for 1 hour or so (or dry in the microwave on HIGH for 2 minutes). Crumble the onions and bun bottoms into a bowl. Add the egg and mix until of a dough-like texture. Cut the steak into 3x5x^{1}/8-inch strips. Place 1 bacon strip, 1 pickle chip and 1 to 2 tablespoons stuffing on each piece of steak and roll to enclose, securing with 2 wooden picks.

Heat the oil in a deep skillet. Combine the flour and seasoned salt in a bowl and coat each roll-up in the mixture. Brown the roll-ups in the oil in the skillet. Transfer to a slow cooker. Shape any leftover stuffing into small patties. Coat with the flour mixture and brown in a skillet. Add to the slow cooker. Stir the remaining flour mixture into 1 cup of the water until smooth. Stir into the hot skillet and cook until thickened, stirring and scraping the bottom to loosen any drippings. Pour over the roll-ups in the slow cooker.

Prepare the gravy mix with the remaining 1 cup water according to the package directions. Pour over the roll-ups in the slow cooker. Cook on HIGH for 3 to 4 hours or until fork tender. Remove the roll-ups and stir the gravy. Remove the wooden picks and serve warm with the gravy, mashed potatoes and peas or spinach. Use the bun tops to sop up the gravy.

Deborah A. Baumann, St. Louis, Missouri

Cravin' Caravan

When I was the pastor of the Greek Orthodox cathedral in Columbus, Ohio, on Easter Sunday each year, after having fasted from meat for forty days, a group of parishioners, my family, and I would leave the resurrection service (which ended at 2:30 a.m.) and head down the street to White Castle, where we would break the forty-day meat fast.

It wasn't just a few people; there were thirty-five to forty cars in the drive-through. So, nearly two hundred people were craving Slyders. Normally, Greeks eat lamb on that night, but we found that Slyders were quick, easy, tasty, and available. Each year for three years, the word got out that Father John was leading the caravan to White Castle.

—*Father John Stavropoulos, Canton, Ohio*

Rolled Castle Steak

2 to 2 1/2 pounds round steak
10 White Castle hamburgers, chopped
1/2 teaspoon curry powder
3 tablespoons vegetable oil
1/2 cup water

Trim the steak of any excess fat and tenderize with a meat mallet. Combine the hamburgers and curry powder in a bowl and mix well. Spread the mixture evenly over the steak and roll to enclose the filling. Tie with kitchen twine or string. Brown the steak all over in the hot oil in a Dutch oven or deep skillet. Reduce the heat to low and add the water. Cook, covered, for 30 minutes, turning occasionally. Use the pan drippings to make gravy, if desired. Makes 4 to 6 servings.

Joyce Walukonis, Florissant, Missouri

Spinach Meat Roll

10 White Castle hamburgers	1/4 teaspoon black pepper
2 eggs	1 (10-ounce) package frozen leaf spinach,
1/3 cup ketchup	thawed and drained
1/4 cup milk	8 ounces thinly sliced cooked ham
1 teaspoon salt, divided	2 cups (8 ounces) shredded mozzarella
1/4 teaspoon dried oregano	cheese, divided

Remove the hamburgers from the buns. Cut or crumble the meat patties into small pieces. Lightly toast the buns and crumble into a bowl.

Preheat the oven to 350 degrees. Beat the eggs in a bowl and stir in the crumbs, ketchup, milk, 1/2 teaspoon of the salt, the oregano and pepper. Add the hamburger pieces and mix well. Pat the mixture into a 10x12-inch rectangle on foil. Spread the spinach over the meat layer, leaving a 1/2-inch border. Sprinkle with the remaining salt. Top with a layer of ham and 11/2 cups of the cheese. Roll up, jelly roll style, starting with a short side and peeling foil away as you roll. Seal the seam and ends; place seam side down on a greased 10x15-inch baking pan.

Bake, uncovered, for 30 to 45 minutes. Top with the remaining cheese and bake for 5 minutes longer or until the cheese is melted.

Carol Miller, Northumberland, New York

In the 1940s, White Castle made a conscious decision to site restaurants within walking distance of large college campuses, which eventually yielded a rich crop of Cravers, especially late at night.

Castle Loaf

12 White Castle hamburgers with
pickles and ketchup
1 pound ground pork
2 garlic cloves, minced
8 sprigs parsley, chopped
1/2 teaspoon black pepper
1/3 cup milk
Pinch of oregano
About 1/2 cup tomato sauce

Preheat the oven to 350 degrees. Place the hamburgers in a food processor fitted with the steel blade and pulse until finely chopped. Combine with the pork, garlic, parsley, black pepper, milk and oregano in a bowl and mix well. Pack the mixture into a greased loaf pan. Pour the tomato sauce over the loaf. Bake for 1 hour. Makes 4 to 6 servings.

Joseph J. Garofalo, Bronx, New York

ERA's (Elaine, Renee & Anthony's) Famous Meat Loaf Recipe

10 White Castle double hamburgers
1 onion, diced
1 egg
1 cup milk
1 tablespoon soy sauce
1 medium tomato, diced
1 teaspoon salt
1 tablespoon sherry
1/2 cup ketchup
1/2 cup brown sugar

Preheat the oven to 350 degrees. Crumble the hamburgers into a large bowl. Add the onion and egg. Stir the milk in gradually. Add the soy sauce, tomato, salt and sherry and mix well. Combine the ketchup and brown sugar in a bowl. Pack the hamburger mixture into a greased loaf pan. Top with the ketchup mixture. Bake for 30 minutes.

Renee Tang, Elmhurst, New York

Meat Loaf Surprise

10 White Castle hamburgers
1¹/₂ pounds ground beef
2 eggs, beaten
¹/₂ cup grated Parmesan cheese
¹/₄ cup chopped green bell pepper
¹/₄ cup chopped onion
1 teaspoon salt
¹/₄ teaspoon garlic powder
¹/₄ teaspoon basil
¹/₄ teaspoon black pepper
Ketchup

Preheat the oven to 350 degrees. Cut the hamburgers into bite-size pieces. Combine the ground beef, eggs, Parmesan cheese, bell pepper, onion, salt, garlic powder, basil and black pepper in a large bowl and mix well. Spread half the ground beef mixture in a 9x13-inch baking dish. Arrange the hamburger pieces on top of the ground beef mixture. Spread with the remaining ground beef mixture. Top with ketchup. Bake for 40 to 50 minutes.

Rachel Faulkner, St. Ann, Missouri

Scientists classify the onion as belonging to the lily family.

Swedish Delight Meatballs

10 White Castle hamburgers
1/2 cup chopped onion
2 strips bacon, cooked and crumbled
1 egg
1/4 cup milk
1/2 teaspoon ground allspice
1/2 teaspoon ground nutmeg
1/4 teaspoon ground ginger
1 tablespoon brown sugar
1/2 teaspoon black pepper

1/2 teaspoon salt
Flour or cornmeal
Vegetable oil or bacon drippings
8 ounces spinach noodles
1 tablespoon butter or olive oil
1 to 11/2 cups water
111/2 teaspoons beef bouillon granules
2 to 3 drops soy sauce
1 teaspoon cornstarch
Fresh dill

Preheat the oven to 250 degrees. Separate the hamburgers from the buns. Toast all the buns on a baking sheet for 12 to 15 minutes or until lightly browned. Cool and pulse into fine crumbs in a food processor. Grind or chop the hamburgers into a bowl and add the onion, bacon, 3/4 of the crumbs, the egg, milk, spices, brown sugar, black pepper and salt and mix well. Shape into 1-inch balls and roll in flour. Brown in oil in a skillet. Set aside and keep warm.

Cook the noodles according to the package directions; drain. Stir in the butter; cover and keep warm. Combine the remaining crumbs, water, bouillon granules and soy sauce in a skillet. Cook for 1 minute, stirring constantly. Stir in the cornstarch and cook for 2 to 3 minutes, stirring constantly. Reduce the heat and add the meatballs. Simmer for 1 minute, stirring to coat. Arrange the noodles on a platter. Cover with the meatballs and sauce. Garnish with dill.

Arlene Gustafson, St. Anthony, Minnesota

Curb service in the 1960s. To compete with other chains offering carhop service, *White Castle brought food out to customers' cars beginning in 1936 and ending in 1972.*

Hamburger Noodle Supreme

10 White Castle hamburgers
8 ounces wide egg noodles
2 cups milk
3 tablespoons all-purpose flour
1 tablespoon beef bouillon granules (3 cubes)
$1/2$ cup canned mushroom pieces

$1/2$ cup condensed cream of mushroom soup
$1/2$ cup sour cream
2 cups frozen chopped broccoli, thawed
$1/2$ cup bread crumbs
$1/4$ cup butter or margarine

Preheat the oven to 375 degrees. Remove the bun tops from the hamburgers and cut the meat patties into bite-size pieces. Cook the noodles in a saucepan until al dente; drain. Combine the milk, flour and bouillon granules in a saucepan and mix well. Cook over medium heat until thickened slightly, stirring frequently.

Combine the mushrooms, soup, sour cream and broccoli in a large bowl and mix well. Add the hamburger pieces and mix gently. Spoon the mixture into a greased 2-quart baking dish. Sprinkle with the bread crumbs and dot with the butter. Bake, covered, for 25 to 30 minutes or until hot and bubbly.

Sandra Manke, Elmhurst, Illinois

Mexicali Stuffed Peppers

3 large green bell peppers
10 White Castle hamburgers, chopped
2 eggs
1/4 teaspoon ground cumin
1/4 teaspoon chili powder
Dash of hot red pepper sauce
1 (16-ounce) jar salsa

Preheat the oven to 350 degrees. Cut the tops from
the bell peppers, removing the stems and seeds.
Combine the hamburgers, eggs, cumin, chili powder
and hot sauce in a large bowl and mix well.
Stuff the mixture into the bell peppers and arrange in
a baking dish. Top with the salsa. Bake, covered,
for 45 minutes.

Ellen Garvey, Bridgewater, New Jersey

Slyder Stroganoff

10 White Castle hamburgers
1 (4-ounce) can sliced mushrooms, drained
4 cups cooked medium noodles
1 (15-ounce) can beef gravy
2 tablespoons sour cream
1 cup plain bread crumbs
3 tablespoons butter or margarine

Preheat the oven to 350 degrees. Cut the hamburgers
into quarters and arrange in a greased 2-quart
baking dish. Spread the mushrooms over the
hamburger quarters. Cover with the noodles.
Combine the gravy and sour cream in a bowl and mix
well. Pour over the noodles. Combine the bread
crumbs and butter in a bowl and mix well. Sprinkle
over the top. Bake for 25 to 30 minutes or until the
bread crumbs are browned. Let stand for
5 minutes before serving.

Ron Knerr, Jeffersonville, Pennsylvania

Hover Crave

I used to be in TV news. As the assignment editor and field producer for Chicago's WLS-ABC TV, I often found myself teaming up with a cameraman and heading out to cover breaking news stories. One hot summer day in 1984, there was a big story breaking about a major prison riot downstate, so the cameraman and I quickly ran to our trusty news helicopter and began our trek to southern Illinois.

We were in the air for about five minutes when hunger struck. With three live broadcasts drawing closer, we knew that landing for food would require two things we didn't have: extra time and an empty field far away from any restaurants.

Then we flew over Berwyn, Illinois, and saw my hometown White Castle at the corner of Harlem and Ogden. Amazingly, I remembered there was an empty field just two blocks away. "Land in that forest preserve field," I ordered the pilot.

I then ran two blocks and ordered twenty-five White Castles, some shakes, and onion rings. I dashed back to the helicopter and we were off again. We ate as we hovered over the riot scene, beaming the live shots back to Chicago. Even a working TV news team has time to feed a White Castle Craving!

—*Gera-Lind Kolarik, Chicago, Illinois*

Disappearing Shrimp de Slyder

10 White Castle hamburgers	1 cup dry sherry
1 pound butter, melted	1/2 cup chopped fresh basil
10 garlic cloves, minced	2 pounds fresh shrimp, peeled and deveined
Juice of 2 lemons	Paprika

Preheat the oven to 350 degrees. Chop the hamburgers into pea-size pieces. Combine the butter, garlic, lemon juice, sherry and basil in a large bowl and mix well. Add the shrimp and hamburgers and stir to coat. Spoon the mixture into a baking dish and sprinkle generously with paprika. Bake for 25 to 30 minutes or until the shrimp have a springy texture when touched with the finger.

Gene Tenner, Naperville, Illinois

*T*o ensure consistent architectural standards, White Castle had nearly all its building components produced by the Porcelain Steel Buildings factory, a White Castle subsidiary, in Columbus.

Here, workers are making the distinctive crenellated turrets. Some stainless steel kitchen fixtures are still manufactured at the company, now called PSB Co.

Shrimp and Snow Pea Castle

10 White Castle cheeseburgers
2 cups chopped peeled cooked shrimp
2 cups sliced snow peas
2 cups drained cooked linguine
1 (10-ounce) can golden mushroom soup
2 cups sour cream
2 eggs, slightly beaten
2 teaspoons minced garlic

1 (8-ounce) puff pastry sheet
10 strips bacon, crisp-fried and crumbled
1/2 cup (1 stick) butter, melted
1 1/2 cups shredded Cheddar cheese
1 1/2 cups shredded mozzarella cheese
1 (2-ounce) can French-fried onions
2 tablespoons pimentos

Preheat the oven to 200 degrees. Remove the cheeseburgers and pickles from the buns. Toast the buns in the oven until dry; crush the toasted buns. Chop the hamburgers and pickles and combine with the shrimp, snow peas, linguine, mushroom soup, sour cream, eggs and garlic in a large bowl.

Increase the oven temperature to 350 degrees. Prepare the puff pastry according to the package directions and place in a greased 7x11-inch baking dish. Bake for 15 minutes or until the pastry begins to puff up. Prick with a fork to deflate.

Pour the cheeseburger mixture into the pastry and bake for 30 minutes. Combine the bacon, butter, cheeses, French-fried onions, pimentos and bun crumbs in a bowl and mix well.

When the cheeseburger mixture begins to set, remove from the oven and spread with the bacon mixture. Return to the oven for 2 to 4 minutes or until the cheese melts.

Stan Nikonowicz, Defiance, Missouri

If all the burgers sold by White Castle since 1921 were laid side by side, they would reach to the moon and back, with plenty left over for lunch!

Stir-Fry with Mushrooms

10 White Castle hamburgers	1 tablespoon oyster sauce
1/4 cup cold water	1 teaspoon vegetable oil
1/4 cup soy sauce	1 tablespoon chopped fresh ginger
2 teaspoons red wine	3 cups sliced fresh mushrooms
4 teaspoons cornstarch	1 cup diagonally sliced green onions
1 tablespoon honey	

Cut the hamburgers diagonally into thin bite-size strips. Combine the water, soy sauce, wine, cornstarch, honey and oyster sauce in a bowl and mix well. Add the hamburger pieces and mix well. Cover and marinate at room temperature for 30 minutes, stirring occasionally. Drain, reserving the marinade.

Preheat a wok over high heat. Add the oil and stir-fry the ginger, mushrooms and green onions until tender-crisp. Remove the vegetables from the wok. Stir-fry the hamburger pieces until browned. Stir the marinade and add to the wok. Cook until thick and bubbly, stirring frequently. Return the vegetables to the wok and heat through. Serve immediately.

Rafael Serrano, New York, New York

The first White Castle building was only fifteen feet by ten feet.

Castle Oriental

10 White Castle hamburgers, no pickles
2 cups cooked rice
1 (15-ounce) can bean sprouts
1 stalk celery, chopped fine
1 medium onion, chopped
1 tablespoon margarine
2 tablespoons soy sauce
1 (10-ounce) can cream of chicken soup
1 (10-ounce) can cream of mushroom soup
1 soup can water

Preheat the oven to 350 degrees. Chop the hamburgers. Combine with the rice and bean sprouts in a large bowl and mix well; set aside. Sauté the celery and onion in the margarine in a medium skillet until tender. Add the soy sauce, soups and water to the skillet and mix well. Pour the mixture over the hamburger mixture. Spoon into a greased 9x13-inch baking dish. Cover with foil and bake for 30 to 40 minutes. Remove the foil for the last 5 minutes of cooking time to allow the casserole to become firm. Makes 4 to 5 servings.

Joy Bandemer, Bolingbrook, Illinois

Castle Sorrel

10 White Castle hamburgers
2 cups chopped fresh sorrel or spinach
1/2 cup chopped onion
1 teaspoon minced garlic
1 (10-ounce) can Cheddar cheese soup
1 (10-ounce) can golden mushroom soup
1 cup sour cream
2 eggs
10 strips bacon, crisp-fried and crumbled
1/2 cup chopped black olives
1/4 cup (1/2 stick) butter

Preheat the oven to 350 degrees. Layer the hamburgers with bottom buns in a greased 9x13-inch baking dish. Set aside the top buns.

Combine the sorrel, onion, garlic, soups, sour cream and eggs in a bowl and mix well. Spread over the hamburgers and bake for 45 minutes or until the top begins to brown. Sprinkle the bacon and black olives over the casserole. Butter the bun tops and warm in a skillet. Top the casserole with the bun tops or serve on the side.

Stan Nikonowicz, Defiance, Missouri

Hawaiian Castle Bake

10 White Castle hamburgers
11 ounces crushed pineapple, drained
1/4 cup uncooked instant rice
2 to 3 tablespoons teriyaki sauce
1 tablespoon lime juice
3 green onions, sliced

1/4 cup macadamia nuts, chopped
1 green bell pepper, cut into thin rings
1 egg, beaten
1 tablespoon sesame seeds
2 to 3 tablespoons grated coconut

Preheat the oven to 350 degrees. Arrange the hamburgers in a single layer with sides touching in a lightly greased 10-inch baking dish. Remove the top buns and set aside.

Combine the pineapple, rice, teriyaki sauce, lime juice, green onions and macadamia nuts in a bowl and mix well. Spoon over the hamburgers. Top with the bell pepper rings. Replace the bun tops and brush with the beaten egg. Sprinkle with the sesame seeds and coconut. Cover with foil and bake for 20 minutes. Remove the foil and bake for 5 to 10 minutes longer or until the coconut is toasted.

Note: For a soft, steamed hamburger that is more traditional, prepare the hamburgers as directed, but steam them in a bamboo steamer over boiling water until the rice is cooked.

TerryAnn Moore, Oaklyn, New Jersey

White Castle first began putting its delicious burgers in boxes in 1931.

Chili Dinner Supreme

10 White Castle hamburgers
3 stalks celery, chopped
1 large green bell pepper, chopped
1 large onion, chopped
2 garlic cloves, minced
2 tablespoons olive oil
1 (10-ounce) can tomato soup
1/2 soup can water
3 ounces sun-dried tomatoes, chopped
(reconstituted, if necessary)

1 teaspoon sugar
1 envelope chili seasoning mix
1 (15-ounce) can dark kidney beans
Mayonnaise
Garlic powder
Grated Parmesan cheese
Chopped onion
Shredded Cheddar cheese

Preheat the oven to 425 degrees. Remove the hamburgers from the buns. Crumble or chop the hamburgers into small pieces. Set aside the buns.

Sauté the celery, bell pepper, onion and garlic in the olive oil in a large skillet. Stir in the hamburger pieces, tomato soup, water, sun-dried tomatoes, sugar and chili seasoning. Simmer for 10 minutes and add the undrained kidney beans. Heat for 5 minutes; keep warm.

Place the bun halves on a foil-lined baking sheet. Spread each with mayonnaise. Sprinkle with garlic powder and Parmesan cheese. Bake for 5 minutes or until hot and bubbly. Serve with the chili, chopped onions and Cheddar cheese.

Mildred Bernhagen, Naperville, Illinois

After the show, at the end of a date, or following the last shift, city dwellers found a quick meal nearby. This night photo was taken in the late 1940s, and though the building says the hamburgers are 5 cents, they had actually increased to 10 cents by this time.

Burger on a Shingle

10 White Castle hamburgers with
extra pickles and onions
3 tablespoons butter
3 tablespoons all-purpose flour
3 cups (or more) milk

1 teaspoon salt, or to taste
1 teaspoon black pepper, or to taste
1 teaspoon ground sage, or to taste
1 sliced green onion for garnish

Remove the hamburgers from the buns, pickles and onions. Cut each hamburger into 9 equal pieces. Set aside the hamburger pieces, buns, pickles and onions.

Preheat the oven to 300 degrees. Heat the butter in a saucepan over medium heat until foamy. Add the flour and mix well. Whisk in the milk gradually until the gravy is smooth and of the desired consistency. Add the salt, black pepper and sage. Cook for 2 minutes and bring to a gentle boil. Cover and simmer for 5 minutes, stirring frequently. Add the hamburger pieces, onions and pickles and simmer, adding additional milk as needed to adjust the consistency. The gravy should be very thick.

Toast the buns on a baking sheet for 15 minutes. (You may want to turn the bottom buns once to toast both sides, as they are moister on the bottom than the top). Place 4 toasted bun halves on a serving plate and top with the gravy. Garnish with the green onion.

Gary Vogel, St. Louis, Missouri

casseroles mom never made

Give Mother a "Night Off" by taking Home a Bag of_

White Castle

HAMBURGERS

Buy 'em by the "Sack"

Castles in Beirut

I was stationed in Beirut in 1982, just a few months
before the massacre of three hundred sleeping Marines in the barracks there.
It was a tense time.

Marines are away from home for long periods of time with few reminders of the familiar,
aside from those precious letters from Mom and Dad and other family members, spouse, or sweetheart.
Loneliness really sets in. One thoughtful deed, however, suggested that someone really did care
about the personnel so far from home.

We had just finished a long and grueling establishment of the perimeter, which included digging foxholes,
running barbed wire, and getting the gun placements into position, when the word was passed,
"The Castles are here!" You would have thought the Grail had appeared! We couldn't believe it:
box after box of White Castle hamburgers. There must have been thousands of them,
at least fifteen for each of the three hundred Marines.

They had been brought frozen from the States, taken to the USS Nashville LPD 13, a support ship docked offshore,
and heated in the ship's many microwaves, then transported by helicopter to the "beach" where we were.

What a day! It was chow call. Every Marine and sailor stopped what he was doing to join the growing line
for a share of this American taste of home. What would have been just another day of anxiety and tension
in a foreign land became a special day for the guys serving their country, a small act of
kindness covered with onions, mustard, and a pickle.

White Castles for everyone! I was there and had my share! Thanks, White Castle!

—Marine Chaplain Captain Herbert M. Goetz, CHC, USN (Ret.),
Command Chaplain U.S. Forces Europe, Columbus, Ohio

Anything Goes Casserole

10 White Castle hamburgers
10 thin slices yellow cheese, any flavor
¹/₄ to ¹/₂ cup any of the next
4 ingredients (optional):
Chopped sautéed onion

Sliced black olives or stuffed green olives
Thinly sliced or chopped bell peppers,
sautéed if desired
Sliced green chiles or jalapeño chiles
1¹/₂ to 2 cups spaghetti sauce

Preheat the oven to 350 degrees. Grease an 8x10-inch baking dish. Arrange the hamburgers evenly in the bottom of the baking dish in 1 layer, overlapping the edges if necessary. Layer the cheese on the buns. Add any optional items to the sauce; spread the spaghetti sauce evenly over the top, covering to the edge of the dish and allowing the sauce to surround the hamburgers. Bake, uncovered, for 20 to 25 minutes or until the sauce is bubbly and the contents are heated through. Serve with tossed salad or raw vegetables and dip.

Recipe doubles well. For a variation, try adding a layer of crumbled tortilla chips before spooning on the tomato sauce. You may also use pizza sauce instead of spaghetti sauce.

Martha S. Schaad, Louisville, Kentucky

Window Shopping

*My old local White Castle was torn down around 1980. It was one of the old-style buildings
with stained glass windows. I've always collected antiques and always wanted one of
those windows, but how in the world could I ever get one? Then along came eBay! About two years ago,
there was a window for sale on eBay and no way was anyone else going to get that window!
The seller called it "a window, possibly from a tavern." I was glad he didn't know what it was. I followed
the bidding until the very last minute and put in a bid I did not think anyone would outbid. Now I own
that original window, and it's one of my most prized possessions. All but one piece of glass is original, and
I had it resoldered as needed and framed so I could hang it in my window. It's a beauty.*

—Ron Fredriksen, Alta Loma, California

*Early White Castle restaurants had very limited
seating, so to sell more burgers, the company
employed the carry-out sack and the slogan
"Buy 'em by the Sack." This is a very early
logo design, probably late 1920s.*

Fabulous Chili Sour Cream Bake

10 White Castle hamburgers
1 can (any size) chili with beans
2 1/2 cups shredded sharp Cheddar cheese, divided
1 (10- to 15-ounce) can enchilada sauce
1 (8-ounce) can tomato sauce
1 small onion, grated or finely chopped
10 to 12 ounces sour cream

Preheat the oven to 375 degrees. Crumble or dice the
hamburgers into a large bowl and set aside. Combine the
chili, 2 cups of the cheese, the enchilada sauce, tomato
sauce and onion. Combine with the hamburgers. Place the
hamburger mixture in a 9x13-inch baking dish. Bake for
20 to 25 minutes. Spread the sour cream and the
remaining cheese over the dish and bake until the cheese
is melted. Serve with corn chips.

Frances Latos-Clarke, Indianapolis, Indiana

A White Castle-shaped spaceship landing pad in Miami! Billy Ingram retired to Miami in 1958 and built three Castles there. The design of this location echoed the space age angles, and the futuristic and glittering glass walls of the many big hamburger chains that had sprung up to compete with White Castle in the late 1950s and early 1960s. The company closed the Florida operations in 1967 due to inefficient supply distribution.

Craver Nacho Casserole

10 White Castle hamburgers
2 (15-ounce) cans chili tomatoes
1 (8-ounce) can tomato sauce
3 (15-ounce) cans mixed pinto and
Great Northern beans
2 envelopes chili seasoning mix

2 bags nacho-flavored tortilla chips, 1 spicy
2 (8-ounce) packages shredded
four-cheese blend
1 (14-ounce) can diced tomatoes, drained
8 ounces sour cream
4 green onions, sliced

Crumble the hamburgers and combine with the tomatoes, tomato sauce, beans and chili seasoning mix in a 3-quart saucepan. Cook over medium heat until the mixture comes to a boil.

Preheat the oven to 375 degrees. Layer the tortilla chips in a glass baking dish. Cover with a layer of the tomato mixture and a layer of the cheese. Repeat the layers until all the ingredients are used. Bake until the cheese is melted.

Spoon the diced tomatoes into the center of the casserole. Top with the sour cream and green onions.

Paul Gaskill, Nashville, Tennessee

Elbows off the table, friends! In 1947, a White Castle photographer shot a series of late night photos known as "the pub series" because they demonstrated that when the bars closed, the White Castle filled up.

10 White Castle Barbecue Shepherd's Pie

10 White Castle hamburgers
1 cup barbecue sauce
4 cups prepared mashed potatoes
1 cup (about 4 ounces) shredded sharp
Cheddar cheese
1 cup heavy cream, whipped

Preheat the oven to 350 degrees. Remove the bun tops from the hamburgers and layer the hamburgers evenly in a greased 9x13-inch baking dish. Spread with the barbecue sauce. Replace the top buns. Cover the hamburgers evenly with the mashed potatoes. Fold the cheese into the whipped cream and spread on the potatoes. Bake for 30 to 35 minutes or until cheese is golden brown.

Carol Krueger, Hickory Hills, Illinois

Double Beef Bake

1 small onion, chopped
Vegetable oil
8 ounces ground beef
1 (15-ounce) can tomato sauce
1 teaspoon sugar
10 White Castle hamburgers
8 ounces mozzarella cheese, shredded

Preheat the oven to 350 degrees. Sauté the onion in the oil in a skillet. Add the ground beef and sauté until brown and crumbly. Add the tomato sauce and sugar and simmer for 20 minutes. Remove from the heat.

Spoon the sauce into the bottom of an 8-inch square baking dish. Arrange 5 hamburgers over the sauce. Top with more sauce, and then another 5 hamburgers. Top with the remaining sauce and the mozzarella cheese. Bake for 20 minutes or until the cheese is melted.

Rebecca Meyers, Indianapolis, Indiana

Part of the 1947 New York series. Carry-out burgers had one drawback — a chronic litter problem in the streets and parking lots around White Castle. The company responded with a new morning duty at each location: employees started the day by picking up the discarded bags and burger boxes until someone had the big idea of putting trash cans in the parking lots.

Calico Casserole

10 White Castle hamburgers
8 ounces bacon, diced
1 small onion, chopped
3/4 cup brown sugar
1/2 cup ketchup
1 tablespoon prepared mustard
1 (15-ounce) can pork and beans
1 (15-ounce) can kidney beans
1 (15-ounce) can lima beans

Preheat the oven to 350 degrees. Remove the meat patties from the buns. Cut or grind the patties into small pieces and set aside. Toast the hamburger buns and crumble or grind.

Brown the meat patties with the bacon and onion until the onion is tender; drain well. Add the bread crumbs, brown sugar, ketchup, mustard and beans. Spoon the mixture into a baking dish. Bake for 45 minutes to 1 hour. Makes 10 servings.

Carol M. Miller, Northumberland, New York

There are more chickens than people in the world.

CHICK FOR PREZ!

Chicken Cheese Castle

This recipe won the grand prize in the 1994 White Castle recipe contest.

10 White Castle cheeseburgers
2 cups chopped cooked chicken breast
1 (10-ounce) can cream of celery soup
2 cups sour cream
1 (4-ounce) jar mushrooms
2 teaspoons minced garlic
2 cups cooked, drained linguine
1 (8-ounce) package puff pastry
1¹/₂ cups shredded provolone cheese

1¹/₂ cups shredded Colby cheese
¹/₂ cup sliced black olives
10 strips bacon, crisp-fried and crumbled
¹/₂ cup (1 stick) butter
1 (2-ounce) can French-fried onions
2 hard-cooked eggs, chopped
¹/₄ cup chopped fresh parsley
1 tablespoon paprika

Preheat the oven to 200 degrees. Remove cheeseburgers and pickles from the buns. Toast the buns in the oven until dry; crumble. Increase the oven temperature to 350 degrees. Chop the hamburgers and pickles and combine with the chicken, celery soup, sour cream, mushrooms, garlic and linguine. Prepare the puff pastry using the package directions and place in a greased 7x11-inch baking dish. Bake for 25 minutes or until the pastry begins to puff up. Prick with a fork to deflate; pour the chicken mixture into the dish and bake for 30 minutes.

Combine the cheeses, black olives, bacon, butter, French-fried onions and bun crumbs. When the top of the chicken mixture is slightly firm, remove from the oven and spread the cheese mixture on top and return to the oven for 2 to 5 minutes or until cheese is melted. Garnish with the eggs, parsley and paprika.

Stan Nikonowicz, Defiance, Missouri

Cheeseburgers first appeared on the White Castle menu in 1962.

Cheeseburger Bake

10 White Castle hamburgers
1 cup chopped onion
2 garlic cloves, chopped
1 (10-ounce) can Cheddar cheese soup
1/2 cup milk
3 chili peppers, diced
1 cup shredded Cheddar cheese

Preheat the oven to 400 degrees. Grease a 9x13-inch baking dish. Remove the top buns and place in the dish. Put the rest of the hamburgers on top of the buns. Add the onions, garlic and chili peppers. Combine the soup and milk in a bowl and mix well, then pour the mixture over the hamburgers. Sprinkle the cheese over all. Bake for 45 minutes.

Harriet Klimek, Newark, New Jersey

Chili Tamale Casserole

This recipe won the grand prize in the 1996 White Castle recipe contest.

10 White Castle hamburgers
2 tablespoons olive oil
1 (13-ounce) jar tamales
2 (15-ounce) cans chili (1 with beans, 1 without)
2 (8-ounce) packages sharp Cheddar cheese, shredded
1 bunch green onions, sliced
Garlic butter

Preheat the oven to 350 degrees. Remove the hamburgers from the buns and crumble into small pieces. Brown the meat in the olive oil in a large skillet until crumbly and crisp. Line the bottom of a greased 9x13-inch baking dish with the tamales. Pour the chili over the tamales. Sprinkle with the cheese, then top with the cooked hamburger meat. Top with the sliced green onions. Bake until hot and bubbly. Place the buns on a foil-lined baking sheet and spread with garlic butter. Broil for 1 to 2 minutes or until toasted. Serve the buns with the casserole. Makes 6 servings.

Carol M. Miller, Northumberland, New York

Macaroni Casserole

2 cups macaroni
1/3 cup chopped red and green bell peppers
1/3 cup chopped onion
2 tablespoons butter
1/4 teaspoon salt
1/4 teaspoon paprika
1 cup evaporated milk
10 White Castle hamburgers
12 slices American cheese

Preheat the oven to 325 degrees. Cook the macaroni using the package directions; drain.

Add the bell peppers, onion, butter, salt, paprika, and evaporated milk to the cooked macroni and mix well. Spoon half of the macaroni mixture into a 9x12-inch baking dish. Remove the top buns from the hamburgers and place the hamburgers with bottom buns face down. Add a layer of 6 slices of cheese. Top with the rest of the macaroni mixture. Layer with the remaining cheese. Top with top buns over the cheese. Bake for 30 minutes.

Gwendolyn Cleasant, Louisville, Kentucky

Three-Cheese Macaroni Crave

10 White Castle hamburgers
2 tablespoons margarine
2 1/2 cups whole milk
1 cup shredded sharp Cheddar cheese
1/2 cup shredded Swiss cheese
8 ounces macaroni, cooked and drained
1 teaspoon each seasoned salt and garlic powder
Black pepper to taste
1/2 cup shredded mozzarella cheese

Preheat the oven to 350 degrees. Separate the meat patties from the buns. Break the bottom buns into small pieces in a bowl. Break the meat patties into pieces in a separate bowl. Cook the bottom buns in the margarine in a skillet. Add the milk and cook until thick, stirring constantly. Stir in the Cheddar and Swiss cheeses and cook until melted. Pour the macaroni into a greased baking dish. Stir the hamburger pieces into the cheese mixture. Stir the cheese mixture and seasonings into the macaroni. Top with the mozzarella cheese. Bake for 30 minutes. Arrange the bun tops in a checkerboard pattern on top of the casserole.

Tim Bosley, Indianapolis, Indiana

By 1968, White Castle had sold over 2 billion hamburgers (2,147,176,733 to be precise).

Bob's Mushroom Casserole

10 to 12 White Castle hamburgers
1 tablespoon butter
4 ounces sliced fresh mushrooms
2 medium diced Roma tomatoes
1 teaspoon hot red pepper sauce
1 teaspoon minced garlic
1 (10- to 12-ounce) jar mushroom gravy
1 order White Castle onion rings,
cut into smaller pieces
2 cups shredded Cheddar cheese

Preheat the oven to 350 degrees. Remove the top buns from the hamburgers and line a baking dish with the bottom buns and hamburgers. Melt the butter in a skillet and sauté the mushrooms, tomatoes, hot sauce and garlic for about 5 minutes. Add the gravy and onion rings and mix well. Pour the gravy mixture over the hamburgers. Top with the Cheddar cheese.

Replace the top portions of the buns and bake for 12 minutes. Or, if you don't want a crunchy bun, leave the bun tops off and replace them after baking.

Bob Sleme, Maryland Heights, Missouri

Cream of Mushroom Burger Bake

10 White Castle hamburgers
1 (10-ounce) can cream of mushroom soup
1/2 cup chopped green bell pepper
1/2 cup chopped onion
1 (2-ounce) can chopped black olives
Melted butter or margarine
1 1/2 cups shredded taco blend cheese

Preheat the oven to 325 degrees. Remove the top buns and set aside. Layer the hamburgers with bottom buns in a 9x13-inch baking dish. Spread the soup over the hamburgers. Sprinkle with the bell pepper, onion and black olives. Replace the top buns and brush with melted butter; sprinkle with the cheese. Bake for 15 to 20 minutes or until the cheese is melted and casserole is heated through. Serve with hot sauce or salsa.

Wynona Bibly, Millstadt, Illinois

Onion Chip Casserole

16 White Castle hamburgers
12 slices American cheese, divided
4 boxes White Castle onion chips, divided
1/4 cup milk

Preheat the oven to 300 degrees. Layer
8 hamburgers top side up in the bottom of a
9x13-inch baking dish. Cover with half the cheese
and half the onion chips. Pour the milk over all.
Place 8 more hamburgers top side down and layer
with the remaining cheese and onion chips. Bake for
25 minutes or until cooked through.

Alaine Lee Cone, Indianapolis, Indiana

Cheesy Burger and Tot Bake

10 White Castle hamburgers
1 (2-pound) bag tater tots, thawed
1 (10-ounce) can Cheddar cheese soup
1 (10-ounce) can cream of celery soup
1 cup shredded Cheddar cheese

Preheat the oven to 350 degrees. Grease a
baking dish. Remove the top buns from the
hamburgers and set aside. Line the baking dish with
the hamburgers and bottom buns. Spread a layer of
the tater tots over the burgers. Combine the soups
and spread half the soup mixture evenly over the tater
tots. Add the top buns and another layer of the tater
tots. Spread with the remaining soup mixture and
sprinkle with the Cheddar cheese. Bake for 20 to
30 minutes or until bubbly and browned.

Bridget Clark, Louisville, Kentucky

A bunch of Forties funsters satisfying their Crave, New York, 1947.

Hash Brown Hot Dish

10 White Castle hamburgers, reserve buns
1 1/2 pounds frozen hash browns, thawed
1/2 teaspoon salt
1 teaspoon black pepper
1 small onion, chopped
2 tablespoons chopped celery
1/3 cup melted butter
1 1/4 cups sour cream
1 (10-ounce) can cream of celery or chicken soup
1 cup shredded Cheddar cheese
1/4 teaspoon hot red pepper sauce (optional)
3/4 cup bread crumbs
Paprika
2 tablespoons chopped chives

Preheat the oven to 350 degrees. Chop the meat patties in a bowl. Stir in the next 6 ingredients. Spread in a baking dish. Mix the sour cream, soup, Cheddar cheese and hot sauce in a bowl. Pour over the hamburger mixture. Toast the buns and crumble. Mix with the bread crumbs and sprinkle over the top of the soup mixture. Sprinkle with paprika. Bake for 35 to 40 minutes or until the casserole is bubbly.
Top with the chives.

Reva Cornett, Independence, Kentucky

Slyder Rally

When I was a ten-year-old in the early 1970s, people were talking about the upcoming 1972 Olympics. Like any young kid growing up in sports-crazy Indiana, I spent most of my free time playing one sport or another, and, of course, basketball ruled.

Now, White Castle had become a pretty important part of my life. My kinfolk in Kentucky would come up and would order thirty to forty White Castle burgers when they visited. I loved those times—all the White Castles a little guy could eat. It was Heaven. But I had to plan a way to get them on my own. So I organized a White Castle derby. My house was four to five miles from the White Castle. My friends and I would race our bikes from our neighborhood to White Castle. The winner could order what he liked (usually four to five hamburgers, a shake, and some fries) and the rest of the field would pick up the tab with allowance or grass-cutting money.

The races became so intense that twelve- to fourteen-year-old boys began entering the derby. The field could sometimes be as many as twenty bikes. The cooks at the White Castle soon knew us and knew about the White Castle Derby. Hardly anything matched the prestige of being the first one through the White Castle doors and having the waitress bring you those five White Castles— no, make that four double hamburgers, fries, and a shake.

I didn't mind the bigger boys entering the derby because they had more pocket money (at least $5 and sometimes even $6). I still won, usually, because that great Castle taste kept my competitive feet turning those pedals.

We raced the White Castle Derby until we were seventeen and eighteen years old, when I went off to the Air Force. I am forty-one now, but you better not race me to a White Castle unless you're willing to pay!

—Timothy Reed, "The Derby King," Indianapolis, Indiana

New York, the classic double date, 1947. Once Americans got a taste for burgers, beef consumption rose quickly, from about 49 pounds per person in 1930 to 53 pounds in 1935. Hamburgers were well established as the country's most popular fast-food meal by the time this photo was taken.

Wrecked Castle Hot Dish

10 White Castle hamburgers
4 cups sliced potatoes
2 cups chopped celery
1 cup sliced onion
1 (15-ounce) can kidney beans
2 (10-ounce) cans condensed tomato soup
Salt and pepper to taste
Melted butter

Preheat the oven to 350 degrees. Remove the top buns and set aside. Line the bottom of a greased baking dish with the bun bottoms. Layer the potatoes, celery, onion, meat patties, kidney beans and soup over the bottom buns. Season with salt and pepper to taste. Cut the tops of the hamburger buns and toss with melted butter. Arrange over the casserole and bake for 1 hour or until the potatoes are soft.

Norma Jean Burdick, Ortonville, Minnesota

O-Layered Mexican Casserole

10 White Castle hamburgers
1 (15-ounce) can chili (no beans)
8 ounces Mexican blend shredded cheese, divided
1 (10-ounce) can diced tomatoes with
green chilies, drained
1 (4-ounce) can sliced black olives, drained
1 cup finely chopped green onions

Preheat the oven to 325 degrees. Grease a large baking dish. Arrange the hamburgers in the dish and spread evenly with the chili. Sprinkle with half the cheese. Spread the tomatoes, black olives and green onions over the chili. Sprinkle with the remaining cheese. Bake for 15 to 20 minutes or until mixture is heated through and cheese is melted and bubbly. Let stand for 3 to 5 minutes before serving.

Renate Siskind, Long Beach, California

Wild and White Rice Casserole

4 tablespoons butter
1 small onion, chopped
1 (4-ounce) can mushrooms, liquid reserved
1 cup chopped celery
1 green bell pepper, chopped
1 (10-ounce) can cream of mushroom soup
1 cup water
3 tablespoons soy sauce
Salt and pepper to taste
1 cup wild rice, cooked
1 cup white rice, cooked
10 White Castle hamburgers, chopped

Preheat the oven to 350 degrees. Grease a rectangular baking dish. Melt the butter in a skillet and sauté the onion, mushrooms, celery and bell pepper until tender. Add the soup, water, soy sauce, salt and pepper and mix well. Add the wild rice, white rice and hamburgers and mix well. Spoon the mixture into the prepared baking dish and bake for 1 hour.

Joan Willy, St. Paul, Minnesota

alla tavola dello castello bianco

Baggage claim to fame

Brian, Vasili, and I woke on a cold morning (18 degrees) and got dressed
to go to the airport for our spring break trip to St. Martin in the Caribbean.
As the spring break excitement was running wild, we decided to wear shorts
and Hawaiian shirts despite the cold.

Since White Castle had introduced the Crave Case, and we'd brought one home, we
all knew we had to do something fun with them. The sturdiness of the case, its looks, and especially
the little luggage tag logo on it gave us an idea. Over the next month, we collected a Crave Case
each and our plan was set: Use the Crave Cases as our carry-on luggage.

So the night before we left, we wrote our own names and addresses in the luggage tag area of the Crave Case
and loaded them with CD players, sunglasses, magazines, and the like before leaving for the airport at 6 a.m.
The response was immediate. We had all been taking bets on how long it would take for someone to say
something about our new Crave-on luggage. On the shuttle to the airport, not three minutes after our first
contact with other people, a lady said, "So, what's with the Crave Case? Are there burgers in there?"
The responses continued from practically everyone we came into contact with.

A group of probably two hundred spring-breakers were in line to check in for a charter flight to Cancún
when we got there. They were all in jeans and sweatshirts and in we strolled with our Hawaiian shirts,
shorts, duffel bags, and Crave Cases. The spring-breakers laughed and asked for Slyders.

Brian was randomly picked by airport security to have his carry-on luggage inspected. One security officer
asked why we didn't bring some burgers for him; the officer who searched the case told Brian,
"I really just wanted to see what you had in there."

On a layover in Philadelphia, where there are no White Castle locations, we got the most questions.
"What is White Castle?" "What is a Crave Case?" "I'm from Columbus and I haven't had a Slyder in years;
do they have them here?" and "Why are you carrying a cardboard box?"
We even had some attractive flight attendants ask about them!

In reality, the Crave Case is a very effective and sensible carry-on. It easily fits in the overhead bins or under the
seat in front of you. It's sturdy enough to carry all of your gear and it is incredibly priced. When you buy a Crave
Case, you get a lightweight, sturdy, spacious carry-on attache, plus thirty steam-grilled burgers as a bonus!

—Jerry Kaltenbach, Columbus, Ohio
Brian Foy, Los Angeles, California
Vasili Trikoupis, Worthington, Ohio

A second generation of grateful Cravers gets a late night burger and coffee at this Castle in the 1940s.

The stoneware cups on the counter at the back are a treasured antique-store find for Castle-iana hunters.

Hurry Up Lasagna

1 (8-ounce) package lasagna noodles
1 (4-ounce) can mushrooms, drained (optional)
1 (28-ounce) jar spaghetti sauce
10 White Castle hamburgers
2 cups (8 ounces) shredded mozzarella cheese
Butter or margarine
Garlic salt to taste

Preheat the oven to 350 degrees. Cook the noodles according to the package directions; drain. Layer half of the noodles in a buttered 1-quart loaf pan. Add the mushrooms to the spaghetti sauce. Pour 1 cup of the spaghetti sauce over the noodles.

Remove the hamburgers from the buns and place 5 patties on the sauce. Sprinkle 1/2 of the mozzarella cheese on top. Add the remaining noodles and repeat the layers. Bake until the cheese melts and starts to brown. Combine butter and garlic salt in a bowl. Brush generously on the buns. Broil until toasted. Serve with the lasagna.

Janet Burns, Westerville, Ohio

Spinach Lasagna

1 (16-ounce) package lasagna noodles
1 small onion, chopped
1 (10-ounce) package fresh spinach
1 teaspoon vegetable oil
Dash each of salt, black pepper and oregano
10 White Castle hamburgers
1 cup shredded mozzarella cheese
1 cup ricotta cheese
1 (28-ounce) jar spaghetti sauce
1 cup crushed potato chips

Cook the noodles according to the package directions; drain. Sauté the onion and spinach in the oil in a skillet and season with salt, black pepper and oregano.

Preheat the oven to 350 degrees. Layer half the noodles, hamburgers, mozzarella cheese, ricotta cheese, spinach mixture and spaghetti sauce in a square baking dish. Repeat the layers. Sprinkle with the crumbled potato chips. Bake for 1 hour and 40 minutes. Serve with a tossed salad and garlic bread. Makes 8 servings.

Julie Sherbondy, Dillon, Colorado

Portobello and Italian Sausage Lasagna

10 frozen White Castle hamburgers
3 tablespoons olive oil
8 tablespoons butter, divided
1 carrot, finely chopped
1 celery stalk, finely chopped
1 medium onion, finely chopped
2 garlic cloves, minced
4 ounces portobello mushrooms, finely chopped

4 ounces Italian sausage, casings removed
Salt and pepper to taste
$1/2$ cup white wine
1 (16-ounce) package lasagna noodles
1 (28- to 32-ounce) jar spaghetti sauce
$1/3$ cup chopped parsley
2 cups shredded Parmesan cheese
15 ounces ricotta cheese
$3/4$ cup milk

Thaw the hamburgers according to the package directions. Separate the hamburgers from the buns and break into small pieces; set aside. Toast the buns until dry and grind to crumbs in a blender or food processor. Heat the olive oil and 3 tablespoons of the butter in a large skillet and sauté the carrot, celery, onion, garlic, mushrooms and Italian sausage over medium heat for 15 minutes. Season with salt and pepper. Add the hamburger meat and cook for 5 minutes. Add the wine and cook for 5 minutes or until the wine is slightly reduced. Add the spaghetti sauce and simmer for 5 to 10 minutes. Stir in the parsley and reduce heat to low. Combine the bread crumbs and Parmesan cheese in a mixing bowl, reserving $1/3$ of the mixture for the topping. Combine the ricotta cheese and milk in a bowl.

Preheat the oven to 375 degrees. Cook the lasagna according to the package directions. Layer the noodles, ricotta mixture, sauce and bread crumb mixture, $1/3$ at a time, in a buttered lasagna dish, ending with the sauce. Melt the remaining 5 tablespoons of the butter in a saucepan. Mix in the reserved bread crumb mixture. Sprinkle over the top. Bake, covered with foil, for 40 minutes. Uncover and bake for 10 minutes longer or until brown. Makes 6 servings.

Lyle Cunningham, Peoria, Illinois

Hi, I'm Beverly, and there's a shy person hiding behind me! Cincinnati, 1967.

All White Castle operators were male until World War II brought about a shortage of men.

Spicy Spaghetti and Meatballs

10 White Castle hamburgers, ground
8 ounces Italian sausage, casings removed
1 teaspoon garlic salt
Pinch of dried basil
1/4 teaspoon red pepper

2 eggs
1 (32-ounce) jar onion and garlic
    spaghetti sauce
Angel hair pasta

Preheat the oven to 350 degrees. Combine the hamburgers, sausage, garlic salt, basil, red pepper and eggs in a large bowl and mix well. Form the mixture into 1 1/2-inch meatballs and arrange in a 9x13-inch baking dish. Cover the dish with aluminum foil and bake for 45 minutes.

Combine the meatballs with the spaghetti sauce in a large saucepan or skillet. Cook the angel hair pasta according to the package directions. Serve the sauce and meatballs over the pasta.

Mary Krejce, Minneapolis, Minnesota

Ultimate Stuffed Pasta Shells

This recipe was the winner of the 1997 White Castle recipe contest.

1 (12-ounce) package jumbo pasta shells
1 pound ground Italian sausage
10 White Castle hamburgers, no pickles
2 cups shredded mozzarella cheese
1 medium Vidalia onion, chopped
1 teaspoon oregano

4 eggs, slightly beaten
1 teaspoon salt
$1/8$ teaspoon black pepper
$1^1/2$ teaspoons crushed fennel seeds, divided
52 ounces garlic-mushroom spaghetti sauce
Grated Romano cheese

Cook the pasta shells according to the package directions; drain. Brown the sausage in a
skillet; drain. Preheat the oven to 350 degrees.

Chop the hamburgers and combine with the mozzarella cheese, onion, oregano, eggs, salt,
black pepper and 1 teaspoon of the fennel seeds in a large bowl and mix well. Stir the remaining
$1/2$ teaspoon fennel seeds into the spaghetti sauce.

Fill the shells with the hamburger mixture. Spread a thin layer of the sauce in a 9x13-inch baking dish.
Arrange the stuffed shells on the sauce. Cover with the remaining sauce and sprinkle with the
Romano cheese. Bake, covered with foil, for 45 minutes. Makes about 38 shells.

Mary-Agnes Korpita, Lafayette, Indiana

This Covington, Kentucky, location, opened January 10, 1997, is in the new split-face block style. The design is an echo of the first Castles, *which also utilized a split-face block construction. Excitingly, it's open 24 hours, so you can admire the style any time of day or night.*

Manicastles

1 (8-ounce) package manicotti shells
10 White Castles hamburgers, chopped
2 eggs, beaten
8 ounces shredded mozzarella cheese
1/4 cup chopped fresh parsley
1/4 teaspoon garlic powder
Salt and black pepper to taste
2 (30-ounce) jars spaghetti sauce
Grated Parmesan cheese

Cook the manicotti shells according to the package directions; drain and rinse. Combine the hamburgers, eggs, mozzarella cheese, parsley, garlic powder, salt and black pepper. Fill the shells with the hamburger mixture. Arrange the stuffed shells in row in a greased baking dish, either one 4-quart or two 2-quart dishes.

Preheat the oven to 350 degrees. Pour the spaghetti sauce over the shells. Sprinkle with the Parmesan cheese. Cover and bake for 30 minutes. Makes 4 to 6 servings.

Mary Jo Marquis, St. Louis, Missouri

Castle Parmigiana

10 to 12 White Castle hamburgers, no pickles, buns removed and set aside
2 cups bread crumbs
1/2 cup Parmesan cheese
1 egg, beaten
10 to 12 slices mozzarella cheese
1 (25-ounce) jar spaghetti sauce
Garlic butter

Preheat the oven to 325 degrees. Combine the bread crumbs and Parmesan cheese in a bowl and set aside. Dip each meat patty in the beaten egg and coat with the bread crumb mixture. Alternate layers of the coated hamburger patties and mozzarella cheese slices in a baking dish. Spread the spaghetti sauce over the top. Sprinkle with the remaining bread crumb mixture. Bake for 30 minutes. Spread garlic butter over the buns. Broil until the butter melts and the buns are toasted. Serve with a green salad.

Judie Williams, El Lago, Texas

Crave-atelli with Garlic Cheese Tops

1 (8-ounce) package manicotti shells	1/2 cup grated Parmesan cheese
1 teaspoon sugar	1 (25-ounce) jar spaghetti sauce, divided
3 cups shredded mozzarella, divided	10 White Castle hamburgers, no pickles
1 (15-ounce) carton ricotta cheese	Butter or margarine
2 eggs	Garlic powder

Cook the manicotti according to the package directions; drain and cool. Preheat the oven to 350 degrees. Combine the sugar, 1 cup of the mozzarella cheese, the ricotta cheese, eggs and Parmesan cheese in a bowl and mix well. Remove the top buns from the hamburgers and chop the hamburgers and bottom buns. Add to the cheese mixture and mix well. Stuff the mixture into the shells.

Spoon half the spaghetti sauce evenly into a 9x13-inch baking dish. Arrange the stuffed shells over the sauce and top with the remaining sauce. Cover and bake for 30 minutes or until hot and bubbly.

Butter the bun tops and sprinkle with the garlic powder and mozzarella cheese, reserving any remaining mozzarella to top the hot stuffed shells. Bake the garlic cheese tops for 10 to 15 minutes. Let stand for 10 minutes before serving.

Richard Potter, St. Louis, Missouri

Trans Craver Airlines

In 1962, I went to work for TWA at the St. Louis airport, loading baggage, cargo, and in-flight meals onto the aircraft. Many of us worked the night shift while we were going to flight school during the day. Our lunch was often White Castle. As we had about 75 people working the late shift, we placed huge orders for several hundred burgers. The local White Castle thought it was a prank the first few times—until we showed up to pay.

Over the years, many coworkers were transferred to different parts of the country and most now live in cities without a White Castle. But the airline maintained a phone system that allowed instant communication throughout the entire network. So during our shift in St. Louis, we would take orders from all over the TWA system and then load the White Castles onto the next flight headed their way.

As word of our little delivery system spread, one of our agents out West decided to throw a White Castle party and ordered 500 burgers. We put them on a plane and a helpful flight attendant kept them in the oven and heated them up just before arrival.

We definitely heard from management on that one though; the passengers could smell the burgers heating in the ovens as that particular flight had no meal service. We were lucky our Slyder system survived after that!

—John Shelly, Miami, Florida

White Castle Pizza

10 White Castle hamburgers
2 tablespoons grated Parmesan
cheese, divided
1/2 teaspoon dried oregano
2 eggs, lightly beaten

1/4 cup milk
2 tablespoons olive oil, divided
3/4 cup pizza sauce
4 ounces shredded mozzarella cheese

Preheat the oven to 425 degrees. Coat a 12-inch pizza pan with nonstick cooking spray. Separate the buns from the hamburgers. Tear the buns into small chunks and place in a bowl. Reserve hamburger pieces.

Combine the torn buns with 1 tablespoon of the Parmesan cheese, the oregano, eggs, milk and 1 tablespoon of the olive oil. Toss with a fork until liquid is absorbed and the bread comes together. Spread the mixture evenly into the prepared pizza pan with a fork. Bake for 7 to 10 minutes or until light brown. Remove from the oven. Spread the sauce over the baked crust. Sprinkle with the mozzarella cheese. Cover with the hamburger pieces. Drizzle the remaining olive oil over the hamburgers. Sprinkle with the remaining Parmesan cheese. Return to the oven and bake 5 to 7 minutes longer or until the crust is brown and the cheese is hot and bubbly. Let stand for 1 to 2 minutes. Cut into 8 wedges. Makes 8 servings.

Mary Ann Lee, Naples, Florida

White Castle employees have younger-looking skin than other people. Further research reveals that the secret is in the steam.

New York Calzone

10 White Castle hamburgers	³/₄ cup shredded mozzarella cheese
³/₄ cup diced green bell pepper	¹/₂ cup grated locateli or Romano cheese
1 cup diced pepperoni or salami	2 egg yolks, beaten
3 garlic cloves, finely chopped	2 tablespoons cornmeal
1 tablespoon olive oil	Olive oil
1 tube refrigerated pizza dough	2 teaspoons garlic powder

Separate the hamburgers from the buns, reserving the top bun and discarding the bottom bun. Sauté the bell pepper, pepperoni and garlic in the olive oil in a small pan over low heat for 10 minutes. Preheat the oven to 350 degrees. Press the pizza dough into a 10x18-inch rectangle on a floured surface.

Crumble the hamburgers and spread lengthwise down the center of the pizza dough. Top with the bell pepper mixture. Sprinkle the cheeses over the the bell pepper mixture.

Fold the bottom edge of the dough over the center and the top edge down to the center, overlapping the bottom edge slightly. Fold the ends of the dough over the top about 1 inch.

Brush the egg yolks over the dough. Make several cuts in the dough for steam to escape. Place the calzone on a greased baking sheet sprinkled with the cornmeal. Bake for 45 minutes.

Arrange the reserved top buns flat side up on a baking sheet. Brush with olive oil and sprinkle with the garlic powder. Bake the calzone for 5 minutes.

Vincent Reilly, New York, New York

Italian Vegetable Bake

10 White Castle hamburgers,
extra pickles and extra onions
1 medium potato, peeled and
cut into 1/2-inch pieces
1 medium sweet potato, peeled and
cut into 1/2-inch pieces
1 red bell pepper, cut into 1/2-inch pieces
2 carrots, peeled and cut into 1/2-inch pieces
5 tablespoons olive oil
Salt and pepper to taste

1 red onion, sliced into thin rings
2 small or 1 large zucchini, cut crosswise
into 1/4-inch slices
2 large ripe tomatoes, cut crosswise
into 1/4-inch slices
1 tablespoon dried parsley
1 tablespoon garlic powder
1/2 cup grated Parmesan cheese
Fresh basil for garnish (optional)

Preheat the oven to 400 degrees. Separate the hamburgers, pickles, onions and buns. Cut the hamburgers into 1/2-inch pieces. Toast the buns and grind into crumbs. Toss the potato, sweet potato, bell pepper, carrots and 2 tablespoons of of the olive oil in a 9x13-inch baking dish. Sprinkle with salt and pepper and toss until coated. Spread the vegetable mixture evenly the dish.

Spread the meat, pickles and onions evenly over the vegetables. Layer the red onion slices evenly over the hamburger mixture. Layer the zucchini evenly over the onions. Drizzle with 2 tablespoons of the olive oil. Sprinkle with salt and pepper. Layer the tomato slices over the zucchini. Combine the parsley, garlic powder, Parmesan cheese, and bun crumbs in a small bowl and mix well. Sprinkle the mixture over the tomatoes. Drizzle with the remaining olive oil. Bake, uncovered, for 40 minutes or until the vegetables are tender and the topping is golden brown. Garnish with fresh basil.
Makes 6 servings.

David Maultsby, Crestwood, Kentucky

slyding along the border

*Many years ago, in a time of disco nightclubs and leisure suits,
I met a lovely girl named Lynda working at a White Castle restaurant.
It was an age when the girls wore dresses, aprons, and the Castle's paper hats.
Boy, did she look cute!*

*Lynda's sister also worked at White Castle, and there she met a friend of my brother, who worked across
the street from the Castle and used to go there for his lunch break. We couldn't have known then that
they would be married in two years. I should have known something was up, even way back when.
However, that is not the way the twist of fate worked out for Lynda and me.*

*We hung out together, stopping at the Castle after a party or cocktails, but we were just good friends.
Time went by and Lynda married and so did I. We remained friends but we didn't stop in at the Castle any longer.*

*Fast forward to 2002. Lynda was driving back from Anchorage, Alaska, where her job had taken her.
She passed through Ohio and stopped at the first White Castle she saw because she had the Crave.
She landed back in New York, divorced, as was I. Always a good friend, she stopped by my home to see
if I had made it through the "crazy days." We went to the Lynbrook Castle and talked about how our dads
would take us there when it had curbside service, real dishes and real cups. Lynda said she had missed
White Castle in Anchorage. We spent a lot of time together and really hit it off!*

*Now at age forty-four, we weren't discussing which party or concert to attend. It was time for the future,
time to plan. So one afternoon I took Lynda to the Lynbrook Castle for lunch. I asked her to marry me,
and to my surprise, she said, "This is so classy, yes." We set the date for January 13, 2003.
We planned a simple civil wedding, but what to do for the reception? The Castle, of course!*

*I visited the Lynbrook Castle to determine whether they could hold a reception for twenty-five to thirty people.
No problem! The management team was most accommodating, and not only did we have reserved seats, we had
waitress service, balloons, two cakes, a gift basket, pictures, and flowers! Everyone was very impressed. I was
asked at the end of the reception, "Why the Castle?" I had a simple reply: "Everyone likes White Castle."*

—Ken and Lynda Muxie, East Rockaway, New York

Slyder Fajitas

1/4 cup orange juice
1/4 cup white vinegar
4 garlic cloves, minced
1 teaspoon seasoned salt
1 teaspoon dried oregano
1 teaspoon ground cumin
1/4 teaspoon black pepper

10 White Castle hamburgers,
   cut into 1/4-inch strips
1 medium onion, thinly sliced
1 medium red bell pepper, thinly sliced
1 tablespoon vegetable oil
4 to 6 (10-inch) flour tortillas, warmed

Combine the orange juice, vinegar, garlic, seasoned salt, oregano, cumin and pepper in a large sealable plastic bag. Add the hamburgers and seal the bag, turning to coat. Set aside.

Sauté the onion and bell pepper in the oil in a skillet until tender-crisp. Remove and set aside. Drain the hamburger mixture and discard the marinade.

Heat the hamburgers in a skillet until very hot, then return the vegetables to the skillet and heat through. Spoon the meat and vegetables onto the tortillas. Serve with shredded cheese, picante sauce and sour cream.

Amber Nay, Indianapolis, Indiana

Castle Enchiladas

This recipe won the grand prize in 1993 White Castle recipe contest.

8 ounces sour cream
4 ounces shredded Cheddar cheese, divided
3 tablespoons chopped parsley
1 envelope taco seasoning mix

10 White Castle hamburgers
1 (16-ounce) jar salsa
1/2 (2-ounce) can sliced black olives

Preheat the oven to 325 degrees. Combine the sour cream, half the cheese and the parsley.

Prepare the taco seasoning mix according to the package directions. Place the hamburgers in a greased 8x12-inch glass baking dish, arranging them side by side in 2 rows. Remove the top bun from each hamburger and spoon the sour cream mixture over the meat patty. Replace the top buns. Spoon any extra sour cream mixture between and around the hamburgers.

Spoon the prepared taco seasoning sauce over each hamburger. Spoon or pour the salsa over and around the hamburgers. Top with the remaining cheese. Dot with the black olives. Bake for 25 to 30 minutes.

Mildred Bernhagen, Naperville, Illinois

Could you pop back inside and bring us some trousers like yours? White Castle began offering curb service in 1935, *which is the approximate date of this photo and ended it in 1972 after the advent of drive-through service.*

Nacho Castle Supreme

10 White Castle hamburgers
1/2 cup finely chopped onions
1 (16-ounce) jar salsa
1 (13-ounce) bag tortilla chips
12 ounces shredded Cheddar cheese
1/4 cup sour cream
1/4 cup sliced black olives

Process the hamburgers with the onions and salsa. Spread the mixture over a bed of the tortilla chips on a microwave-safe platter. Sprinkle with the cheese and microwave for 2 to 2 1/2 minutes. Spread the sour cream on top and garnish with the black olive slices.

John Stewart, Toledo, Ohio

Castle Nacho Grande

1 (16-ounce) jar salsa
8 ounces shredded Cheddar cheese
1 medium onion, chopped
10 White Castle hamburgers
10 to 25 chopped black olives
1 (16-ounce) can nacho cheese
Shredded lettuce
2 chopped tomatoes
8 ounces sour cream
1 (20-ounce) bag tortilla chips

Preheat the oven to 350 degrees. Spread 1/3 of the salsa over the bottom of a 9x13-inch pan. Sprinkle with 1/2 cup of the Cheddar cheese and some of the chopped onion. Cut each hamburger and bun into 4 to 6 pieces and arrange on top of the salsa layer. Top with the remaining salsa, Cheddar cheese, the onion and black olives. Pour the nacho cheese over all and bake for 15 to 20 minutes. Let stand for 5 minutes to cool. Top with lettuce, the chopped tomatoes, more onions, more shredded cheese, black olives and sour cream. Serve with tortilla chips.

Don Marsh, Indianapolis, Indiana

Building a fast food culture, one Craver at a time. The white hats worn by operators were designed by Billy Ingram and produced by the Paperlynen company, a White Castle subsidiary.

Castle Belle Grande

2 (13-ounce) bags tortilla chips
2 (16-ounce) cans refried beans
10 White Castle hamburgers
1 pound ground beef
1 envelope taco seasoning mix
1 (8-ounce) package shredded taco cheese
1 (16-ounce) can nacho cheese
Shredded lettuce
4 tomatoes, chopped
1 (2-ounce) can black olives
1 (8-ounce) bottle taco sauce
8 ounces sour cream

Preheat the oven to 400 degrees. Bake the tortilla chips on a baking sheet for 5 to 10 minutes. Heat the refried beans until heated through, stirring frequently. Microwave the hamburgers until hot and tear the meat into pieces. Cook the ground beef in a skillet until brown and crumbly; drain. Stir in the taco seasoning. Spoon over the tortilla chips. Top with the hamburger pieces. Spread the taco cheese over the meat, then top with the refried beans and nacho cheese. Garnish with lettuce, the tomatoes, olives, taco sauce and sour cream.

Debbie White, Indianapolis, Indiana

Tortilla Turrets

10 White Castle hamburger patties
Vegetable oil
4 (6-inch) tortillas
1/2 cup mild chunky salsa
8 ounces Cheddar cheese, cubed
1/2 cup ketchup
1 cup sour cream

Brown the hamburger patties in the oil in a skillet. Cut into strips and set aside. (Cube the buns and toast for croutons for later use in salads.) Sauté the tortillas in the skillet and set aside. Combine the salsa and cheese and set aside.

Preheat the oven to 375 degrees. Place the tortillas on a lightly greased baking sheet. Spread the ketchup over the tortillas. Mound the meat strips on the tortillas so they are higher in the center. Cover with the salsa mixture so that it is higher in the center. Bake until the cheese bubbles. Top with sour cream, shaping it so it points upward.

Lillian Fisher, Tucson, Arizona

from an Idea
to
**A NATIONAL
INSTITUTION**
-through
constant
striving to
improve

**White Castle
HAMBURGERS**

BUY 'EM BY THE "SACK"

Castillo Blanco Tacos

10 White Castle hamburgers, chopped
1/2 head lettuce, shredded
1/2 tomato, diced
1/4 to 2 teaspoons taco seasoning mix, or to taste
10 taco shells
1 cup shredded cheese

Combine the hamburger pieces, lettuce, tomato
and taco seasoning in a bowl. Taste and
adjust the seasoning if needed. Fill each taco
shell equally with the hamburger mixture.
Top each taco with some of the cheese.

Jill Strub, Cincinnati, Ohio

Taco Pie

10 White Castle hamburgers, no pickles
1 cup salsa
1 envelope taco seasoning mix
1 small white onion, chopped
1 (2-ounce) can chopped black olives
2 cups shredded Cheddar cheese, divided
1 cup sour cream
1 unbaked (9-inch) pie shell

Preheat the oven to 350 degrees. Chop the
hamburgers into small pieces. Combine with the
salsa, taco seasoning, onion, black olives,
1 cup of the Cheddar cheese and sour cream in a
large bowl and mix well. Spoon the mixture into the
pie shell and top with the remaining cheese.
Bake for 25 minutes or until the pie shell is
browned and the mixture is hot.

Tiffany Shain, Louisville, Kentucky

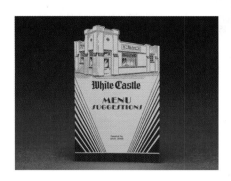

Taco Bake

8 ounces ground beef
Vegetable oil
1/2 small onion, chopped
1/2 teaspoon garlic powder
1/2 (6-ounce) envelope taco seasoning mix
1/2 (4-ounce) can tomato sauce
1/2 cup cottage cheese
1/2 cup sour cream
10 White Castle hamburgers, cut into fourths
2 cups shredded Monterey Jack cheese
1 cup crushed tortilla chips

Preheat the oven to 350 degrees. Brown the ground beef in a little oil in a skillet; drain. Add the onion, garlic powder, taco seasoning and tomato sauce and set aside. Combine the cottage cheese and sour cream in a bowl and set aside. Arrange half the hamburger pieces in the bottom of a greased 2 1/2-quart baking dish. Layer half the ground beef mixture and half of the sour cream mixture on top. Sprinkle with half the Monterey Jack cheese. Repeat the layers and top with the remaining cheese. Bake, uncovered. for 30 to 35 minutes. To serve, sprinkle with the tortilla crushed chips.

Jill Strub, Cincinnati, Ohio

Taco Surprise

1 pound ground beef or ground chuck
1 bunch green onions, sliced
1 1/2 teaspoons salt
1 teaspoon black pepper
1 envelope taco seasoning mix
10 White Castle hamburgers
8 ounces shredded Cheddar cheese
Chopped fresh tomato
Ranch salad dressing, sour cream and lettuce

Cook the ground beef and sliced green onions in a skillet over medium heat until the onions are well done, reserving some of the green onions for garnish; drain. Add the salt, black pepper and taco seasoning according to the taco seasoning directions. Let stand to cool. Preheat the oven to 350 degrees. Remove the top buns from the hamburgers and set aside. Arrange the hamburgers with bottom buns in a 9x12-inch baking dish. Spread the ground beef mixture over the hamburgers. Top with the cheese. Replace the top buns. Bake for 20 to 25 minutes. Let stand for 10 minutes. Garnish with green onions and fresh tomatoes. Serve with ranch dressing, sour cream and lettuce, if desired.

Audie Dixon & family, Louisville, Kentucky

Fish sandwiches were first added to the White Castle menu in 1955.

South-of-the-Border Castles

10 White Castle hamburgers
2 (8-ounce) packages cream cheese, softened
1 (15-ounce) can chili without beans
1 (4-ounce) can chopped green chiles
8 ounces shredded Cheddar cheese
Salsa and refried beans

Preheat the oven to 350 degrees. Remove the top buns from the hamburgers and set aside. Arrange the hamburgers with bottom buns in a large rectangular baking dish. Spread the cream cheese over the meat and replace the top buns, pressing down on the buns. Spoon the chili over the hamburgers. Scatter the green chiles over the top. Sprinkle with the cheese. Bake until the cheese melts. Serve with salsa and refried beans.

Maude R. Hopkins, Old Hickory, Tennessee

Southwest Crave Casserole

12 White Castle hamburgers with pickles
1 tablespoon olive oil
1 medium red bell pepper, diced
1 garlic clove, minced
1 teaspoon ground cumin
1 cup salsa
1 (15-ounce) can black beans, drained
1 (11-ounce) can Mexicorn, drained
8 ounces shredded sharp Cheddar cheese
1/2 cup sour cream
Chopped fresh cilantro
Additional sour cream

Preheat the oven to 350 degrees. Place the hamburgers in 2 rows in a greased baking dish. Heat the olive oil in a medium skillet over medium heat. Sauté the bell pepper and garlic until tender-crisp. Add the cumin, salsa, black beans and corn and heat through. Remove from the heat and stir in 1 cup of the cheese and the sour cream. Pour the mixture over the hamburgers. Sprinkle with the remaining cheese. Bake for 20 to 25 minutes or until bubbly. Top with chopped cilantro and a dollop of sour cream.

Marge Walker, Santa Claus, Indiana

Fit for a King Ring

10 White Castle hamburgers, top buns removed
1 (6-ounce) package burrito seasoning mix
1 cup shredded Mexican four-cheese blend
1 tablespoon all-purpose flour
2 tablespoons water
2 (8-ounce) packages refrigerator crescent roll dough
2 tablespoons butter or margarine

1/2 teaspoon minced garlic
1 teaspoon dried cilantro
1/4 teaspoon salt (optional)
3 tablespoons shredded Mexican four-cheese blend
2 tablespoons diced green bell pepper
1/2 cup salsa
2 tablespoons sour cream

Preheat the oven to 375 degrees. Chop the meat patties, pickles and bottom buns coarsely. Add the burrito seasoning mix, 1 cup Mexican cheese, the flour and water and mix well, using hands if needed.

Arrange the 16 crescent dough triangles in a circle with bases overlapping in the center and points to the outside, forming a 5-inch diameter circle in the center, on an ungreased 12-inch pizza pan. Press down along the base with fingers to flatten to a 1/4-inch thickness. Spoon the hamburger mixture evenly around the dough base. Fold the triangle points over the hamburger mixture and tuck under base at center. The mixture will not be completely covered. Bake for 20 to 25 minutes or until golden brown.

Cut the bun tops into bite-size pieces. Heat the butter in a small nonstick skillet over medium heat. Sauté the bun pieces and minced garlic in the butter until the bun pieces are browned. Remove from the heat and stir in the cilantro and salt. To serve, place browned bun pieces in the center of the ring. Sprinkle with 3 tablespoons Mexican cheese and the bell pepper. Spoon the salsa over all and top the bun pieces with sour cream. Serve with additional salsa and sour cream if desired. Makes 8 servings.

Gloria K. Herdman, Pomeroy, Ohio

Everyone from a lanky Hollywood extra to Auntie Em loves 'em. Customers with fond lifelong memories of White Castle gave the chain an especially deep and loyal following that allowed White Castle to survive the Depression, World War II, and the "burger wars" of the 1970s that finished off many of its competitors.

Castilla Tortilla Pie Casserole

1 cup diced black olives
1 cup diced jalapeño chiles
1 (15-ounce) can corn
$1/2$ teaspoon salt
$1/2$ teaspoon pepper
10 White Castle hamburgers, no pickles

1 (26-ounce) jar enchilada sauce
3 (8-inch) corn tortillas
$2 1/4$ cups shredded cheese
   ($1/2$ Monterey Jack, $1/2$ sharp Cheddar)
Whole jalapeño chiles

Preheat the oven to 350 degrees. Combine the black olives, 1 cup jalapeño chiles, the corn, salt and pepper in a bowl. Cut the hamburgers into quarters and set aside.

Brush the bottom of an 8- to 9-inch casserole with enchilada sauce. Place 1 tortilla in the dish. Arrange quarters of 5 hamburgers on the tortilla. Layer 1 cup of the olive mixture, about $3/4$ cup of the enchilada sauce and $3/4$ cup of the grated cheese on top. Repeat the layers of tortilla, hamburger quarters, olive mixture, enchilada sauce and cheese until all the ingredients are used, ending with the cheese.

Cover the dish and bake for 35 to 40 minutes. Let stand for 5 minutes before serving. Garnish with whole jalapeños.

Bob Stastny, Los Angeles, California

Castle Rellenos

10 medium poblano or Anaheim chiles	1 cup all-purpose flour
10 White Castle hamburgers, pickles optional	5 eggs, beaten
6 ounces Monterey Jack or sharp Cheddar cheese, sliced	1 large onion, chopped
Vegetable oil	2 garlic cloves, minced
	2 jalapeño chiles, seeded and minced
	1 (28-ounce) can tomatoes, chopped

Preheat the oven to 400 degrees. Roast the peppers until the skins char and blister, turning occasionally. Place the peppers in a paper or plastic bag to cool. Peel off the skins and slit the peppers slightly, removing the seeds. Cut the hamburgers into halves. Place 2 hamburger halves and 1 cheese slice in each pepper.

Heat enough oil to measure 1 inch in a skillet. Coat the stuffed peppers in the flour, then dip in the eggs. Fry the peppers in the hot oil until browned, turning occasionally; drain. Heat 3 tablespoons oil in a saucepan and sauté the onion, garlic and jalapeño chiles until the onion is tender. Add the tomatoes and cook until the mixture reaches a sauce consistency. Serve over the rellenos.

Joshua Goodman, White Plains, New York

Index

Index

Index

Index

www.whitecastle.com